FIT
FOR
SERVICE

NAVIGATING THE CROSSROADS OF FITSM AND ITSM FOR SEAMLESS IMPLEMENTATION

NAZA SEMENOFF

CONTENTS

FOREWORD

I n today's fast-paced, technology-driven, and ever-changing business landscape, organizations face numerous challenges in delivering high-quality services to their customers. The demand for efficient, effective, and value-driven service management practices has never been greater. This book is dedicated to all the professionals and organizations who are striving to optimize their service management practices and align them with industry best practices.

Both FitSM and ITSM (IT Service Management) are methodologies that aim to streamline and optimize IT service provision within organizations. In this chapter, we will explore the fundamentals of FitSM and ITSM, their goals, and the importance of adopting these practices.

What is FitSM and ITSM?

FitSM, short for "Federated IT Service Management," is a lightweight and pragmatic framework designed to assist organizations in implementing effective and efficient service management practices. It is specifically tailored for smaller organizations or those just starting on their ITSM journey. FitSM provides a streamlined approach to IT service management, focusing on the essential aspects without unnecessary complexity.

ITSM, or "IT Service Management," refers to the discipline of managing IT services in a way that ensures the delivery of value to customers. It encompasses various processes, tools, and methodologies aimed at improving service delivery, achieving customer satisfaction and optimizing resource utilization within IT organizations.

This book explores the intersection of FitSM and ITSM and how organizations can leverage these frameworks to enhance their service management capabilities.

Who is this Book For?

This book is intended for professionals in IT service management, including IT managers, service delivery managers, IT consultants, and IT practitioners. It is also relevant for organizational leaders and decision-makers who are responsible for driving service management transformation within their organizations.

What will be Covered?

Throughout the following chapters, we will cover a wide range of topics related to FitSM and ITSM implementation. Here's an extended overview of what you can expect:

Chapter 1: Introduction to FitSM and ITSM: In this chapter we embark on an explorative journey into the realms of FitSM and ITSM, two pivotal frameworks in the IT service management arena. Beginning with a historical dive into FitSM's origins, the chapter unfolds its foundational principles and key components, from service management systems to risk management. The contrasts and comparisons between FitSM and ITSM are elucidated, highlighting their unique and overlapping benefits. Moreover, the chapter emphasizes the tangible advantages of implementing these frameworks, such as improved service delivery and customer satisfaction. Concluding with a segment on training and certification, readers are equipped with insights into the importance and benefits of professional development in the world of IT service management.

Chapter 2: Understanding the Crossroads: In Chapter 2, we find ourselves at the many crossroads of decision-making pivotal to a successful FitSM and ITSM journey. The chapter dissects the intricate process of selecting the right ITSM framework, weighing the adaptable nature of FitSM against other heavyweights like ITIL®, COBIT, and ISO 20000. Beyond the selection of a framework, readers will confront the challenging debate of outsourcing versus retaining IT services in-house, considering both the potential rewards and inherent complexities. The chapter also delves deep into the art of prioritization, emphasizing the role of continuous improvement and alignment with critical business objectives. A recurring theme of the chapter is the profound impact of organizational change, guiding readers through strategies to ensure seamless adoption and overcome resistance. Finally, an eye to the future is maintained throughout, emphasizing the significance of sustainability and scalability in an ever-evolving landscape. As we navigate these crossroads, the chapter underscores the importance of informed decisions, ensuring FitSM and ITSM implementations are tailored to drive organizational success.

Chapter 3: Challenges in FitSM and ITSM Implementation: Chapter 3 delves into the challenges organizations face when implementing FitSM and ITSM frameworks. From leadership commitment to employee resistance and training gaps, the chapter underscores the multifaceted nature of these obstacles. It stresses the significance of clear communication, comprehensive training, and setting realistic expectations.

Emphasis is also placed on the need for continuous improvement to ensure lasting benefits. By addressing these challenges head- on, organizations can enhance their chances of a successful implementation, leading to service quality improvements and cost efficiencies.

Chapter 4: Getting Started with FitSM: A Step-by-Step Guide: This chapter provides readers with a comprehensive guide to implementing the FitSM framework, a lightweight IT service management standard designed for practicality and efficiency. Beginning with an introduction to FitSM's principles and objectives, the chapter sequentially details the steps essential for its successful adoption. These steps range from understanding the framework's core concepts, assessing current IT practices, and setting clear implementation goals, to building a dedicated project team, customizing the framework to an organization's unique needs, and seeking external validation through certification. Emphasizing the importance of communication, stakeholder engagement, continuous improvement, and the potential value of external support, the chapter acts as a roadmap for organizations aspiring to establish or refine their IT service management practices using FitSM.

Chapter 5: The Dark Sides of FitSM: Navigating Potential Pitfalls: In Chapter 5, the narrative pivots to address the potential challenges and pitfalls associated with the FitSM framework.

Recognizing that no system is perfect, the chapter delves deep into the potential issues organizations might encounter when adopting FitSM. Key challenges explored include the dangers of over-standardization, complexities in larger organizational structures, the potential bureaucracy of excessive documentation, and the initial costs of adopting the framework. The chapter not only identifies these pitfalls but also provides actionable solutions to navigate them, ensuring that organizations can make the most of FitSM without being encumbered by its limitations. Concluding on a pragmatic note, the chapter underscores that while FitSM is a valuable tool, its success hinges on thoughtful implementation and ongoing evaluation.

Chapter 6: Case Studies: Successful FitSM Implementation: Chapter 6 delves into several real-world case studies of organizations that have implemented either FitSM or ITSM. These narratives spotlight the distinct advantages, challenges, and experiences encountered by different businesses, offering insights into the suitability of each framework based on specific organizational needs. Comparatively, FitSM emerges as a more agile, adaptable, and user-friendly approach, especially favored by businesses with a lean methodology. In contrast, ITSM is presented as a robust, comprehensive system, ideal for larger entities seeking structure and standardized processes. The chapter underscores the importance of choosing a framework aligned with an organization's operational style and objectives.

Chapter 7: Future of FitSM: Emerging Trends and Opportunities: Chapter 7 delves into the evolving trajectory of FitSM in IT service management. It emphasizes the integration of AI and Machine Learning, promising enhanced automation and decision-making. The chapter highlights the need for agility in service delivery, embracing methods like Agile and DevOps. With multiple service providers in modern IT, Service Integration and Management (SIAM) ensures coordinated delivery.

Cybersecurity's heightened role within FitSM is underscored, emphasizing proactive measures and compliance. In essence, the future of FitSM is painted as innovative and crucial for businesses navigating the dynamic digital realm.

Chapter 8: Tips for Successful FitSM Implementation: This chapter emphasizes the importance of a strategic approach to FitSM implementation. Gaining top management's support is vital, as is setting clear objectives that align with the organization's goals. Organizations are encouraged to assess their readiness and tailor FitSM to their specific context. Continuous monitoring, celebrating successes, ensuring scalability, fostering collaboration, and harnessing technology are vital components.

External support can be beneficial for expertise and accelerating the process. The aim of this book is to equip readers with the knowledge, tools, and strategies needed to implement FitSM and ITSM effectively within their organizations. We will provide practical guidance, expert insights, and real-world examples to help drive positive change and achieve service management excellence.

Now, let's dive deep into the world of FitSM and ITSM implementation and embark on this transformative journey together!

ABOUT THE AUTHOR

With an MBA complementing her robust background in ITSM, Naza Semenoff stands as a testament to dedication in the ITSM realm. Beyond her academic achievements, her notable certifications, including the ITIL v3 Expert, highlight her commitment to perpetual learning and meaningful contributions within the ITSM domain.

Throughout her illustrious journey, Naza has collaborated with an array of clients spanning sectors such as finance, healthcare, academia, and technology. These partnerships, each unique in its challenges and goals, have emphasized the significance of melding best practices with the specific contours of an organization.

While her profound grasp of ITIL, a premier standard for ITSM, plays a pivotal role in her ventures, Naza emphasizes the essence of customization — ensuring ITIL's principles align with the distinct visions and challenges of every institution she collaborates with.

In the ever-shifting sands of ITSM, staying updated is paramount. Naza's MBA and consistent interactions within industry forums position her at the vanguard of the ITSM evolution. Beyond her consultancy, she channels her insights into writings, hoping to ignite discussions, inspire innovative viewpoints, and tap into the collective genius of the ITSM world.

For Naza Semenoff, every ITSM endeavor represents a dual opportunity: to impart knowledge and to imbibe new insights.

Each project becomes a beacon of collaboration, illuminating the complexities of IT Service Management for all stakeholders.

CHAPTER 1

INTRODUCTION TO FITSM AND ITSM

n this chapter, we will delve into the world of FitSM and ITSM, exploring the fundamental concepts and principles that underpin these frameworks. FitSM, which stands for "Federated IT Service Management," is a lightweight and pragmatic approach aimed at facilitating service management in IT service provision, including federated scenarios. ITSM, on the other hand, refers to the practice of aligning IT services with the needs and goals of the business to ensure smooth operations and customer satisfaction.

1.1. Overview of FitSM

1.1.1. Origin of FitSM

FitSM, funded by the European Commission and licensed under a Creative Commons Attribution 4.0 International License, offers a structured approach to ITSM. It is designed to be lightweight and adaptable, making it suitable for a wide range of IT service providers. The FitSM standards family includes various parts, from an overview and vocabulary (FitSM-0) to detailed implementation guides (FitSM-5) and maturity assessments (FitSM-6).

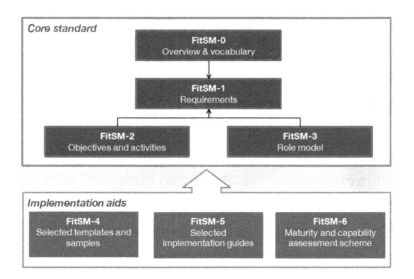

At the heart of FitSM is the concept of ITSM, which involves planning, delivering, operating, and controlling IT services. These services are structured to provide value to customers by aiding them in achieving desired results. A Service Management System (SMS is central to this, encompassing policies, processes, roles, and procedures.

Principles of FitSM

FitSM's process model includes various ITSM processes like Service Portfolio Management (SPM), Service Level Management (SLM), and Service Reporting Management (SRM). The model emphasizes continual improvement through the Plan-Do-Check-Act cycle. FitSM is built upon a set of core principles:

- Customer Focus: FitSM emphasizes understanding and meeting the needs of customers and stakeholders to ensure the delivery of valuable IT services. This principle highlights the importance of constantly assessing customer requirements and aligning service offerings with them.

- Continuous Service Improvement: FitSM encourages organizations to continually improve their IT services through feedback, analysis, and optimization. This principle emphasizes the need for a proactive approach to identify areas for improvement and initiate relevant actions.

- Process Efficiency: FitSM promotes the efficient and effective execution of IT service management processes to deliver high-quality services. This principle emphasizes the importance of eliminating waste, streamlining processes, and optimizing resource allocation.

- Simplicity: FitSM follows a minimalist approach, focusing on essential processes, roles, and activities. By eliminating unnecessary complexity, organizations can adopt and integrate FitSM more easily into their existing structures. Simplicity also enhances the clarity and transparency of service management practices. FitSM achieves simplicity by providing a concise set of processes and avoiding unnecessary bureaucratic overhead. This allows organizations to establish a lean yet effective service management framework.

- Flexibility: FitSM is designed to be flexible, enabling organizations to adapt and customize its processes and practices to meet their specific requirements. This adaptability allows organizations to respond quickly to changes in business needs and market demands, ensuring agility and competitiveness. FitSM's flexibility manifests through its modular design, which allows organizations to select and implement only the components that align with their specific needs. Whether an organization is small or large, private, or public, FitSM can be tailored to ft its unique circumstances.

- Cost-effectiveness: FitSM ensures cost-effective service management by focusing on key components that provide the most value. By avoiding unnecessary processes and practices, organizations can optimize resource utilization and reduce unnecessary expenses associated with implementing and maintaining service management practices. This cost- effectiveness is particularly beneficial for smaller organizations with limited resources. FitSM achieves this by promoting a pragmatic approach, where organizations can prioritize and select the most impactful processes and activities within their available constraints.

- Integration with other frameworks, such as project management, risk management, and quality management, enables organizations to achieve a holistic approach to service delivery, ensuring consistency and alignment across different processes and functions. FitSM encourages organizations to break down the silos between departments and establish cross-functional collaboration, leading to improved efficiency and effectiveness in service management practices.

1.2. Key Components of FitSM

1.2.1. Service Management System (SMS)

In the FitSM framework, the SMS takes center stage as a pivotal and central component. It serves as the linchpin for orchestrating and managing IT services, providing a well-structured and organized framework that delineates the roles, responsibilities, and processes integral to service delivery. The SMS plays a multifaceted role, ensuring that all facets of service management are not only meticulously documented but also meticulously controlled and subject to continuous improvement efforts. It serves as a reservoir of knowledge and a beacon of guidance, illuminating the path for effective and efficient service management activities.

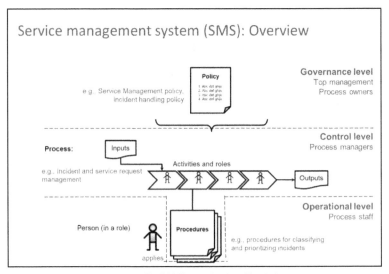

Source: FitSM Foundation Training

The core of FitSM is its set of standards, which are divided into several parts, each focusing on different aspects of IT service management. The main part, FitSM-0, provides an overview of the family, while FitSM-1 contains the core requirements.

17 general requirements are organized into 7 distinct categories. They form the foundation of an effective SMS, ensuring that the overarching management framework is robust and comprehensive. 65 Process-Specific Requirements for an SMS are aligned with the FitSM process model as detailed in FitSM-0 and are categorized into 14 groups. They address the specific operational aspects of ITSM, ensuring that each process is executed with precision and efficiency.

These requirements cover a range of IT service management aspects, including service planning, delivery, relationship management, control, resolution, and release. They are designed to be minimal, achievable, and pragmatic, making FitSM suitable for organizations that might find other ITSM frameworks too complex or resource intensive.

As evident below, each requirement in FitSM is stated in a clear and concise manner, making it easy for organizations to understand what is needed to comply with the standard. The requirements are designed to be applicable to a wide range of IT service providers, regardless of their size or the nature of the services they provide.

The following is a comprehensive list of the requirements as per the FitSM standards series, providing a detailed roadmap for organizations seeking to enhance their IT service management capabilities in line with globally recognized best practices.

General requirements for a service management system

GR1 Top Management Commitment & Accountability (MCA)

REQUIREMENTS

- GR1.1 A member of top management of the service provider(s) involved in the delivery of services shall be assigned as the SMS owner to be accountable for the overall SMS.
- GR1.2 A general service management policy shall be defined that includes overall service management goals as well as a commitment to continual improvement and a service- oriented and process-oriented approach. The service management policy shall be approved and communicated to relevant parties by the SMS owner.
- GR1.3 The SMS owner shall conduct management reviews at planned intervals.

GR2 Documentation (DOC)
REQUIREMENTS

- GR2.1 The key elements of the SMS shall be documented to support effective planning. This documentation shall include the SMS scope statement (see GR3), the general service management policy (see GR1) as well as the service management plan and related plans (see GR4).
- GR2.2 Documented definitions of all service management processes (see PR1-PR14) shall be created and maintained. Each of these definitions shall include:

  o Description of the goals of the process
  o Description of the inputs, activities and outputs of the process
  o Description of process-specific roles and responsibilities
  o Description of interfaces to other processes
  o Related process-specific policies as needed
  o Related process- and activity-specific procedures as needed

- GR2.3 The key outputs of all service management processes (see PR1-PR14) shall be documented, and the execution of key activities of these processes recorded.
- GR2.4 Documented information shall be controlled, addressing the following activities as applicable:

  o Creation and approval
  o Communication and distribution
  o Review
  o Versioning and change tracking

GR3 Scope & Stakeholders of IT Service Management (SCS)

REQUIREMENTS

- GR3.1 The stakeholders of the IT services and the SMS shall be identified and their needs and expectations analysed. Relevant legal, regulatory and contractual requirements shall be considered.
- GR3.2 The scope of the SMS shall be defined taking into consideration the results from the stakeholder analysis.

GR4 Planning IT Service Management (PLAN)

REQUIREMENTS

- GR4.1 A service management plan shall be created and maintained. It shall include:

  o Goals and timing of implementing or improving the SMS and the related processes
  o Roles and responsibilities
  o Training and awareness activities
  o Technology (tools) to support the SMS
- GR4.2 Any plan shall be aligned to the overall service management plan and other plans as needed.

GR5 Implementing IT Service Management (DO)
REQUIREMENTS
• GR5.1 The service management plan shall be implemented. • GR5.2 Within the scope of the SMS, the defined service management processes shall be followed in practice, and their application, together with the adherence to related policies and procedures, shall be enforced.

GR6 Monitoring And Reviewing IT Service Management (CHECK)
REQUIREMENTS
• GR6.1 The effectiveness of the SMS and its service management processes shall be measured and evaluated based on suitable key performance indicators in support of defined or agreed goals. • GR6.2 Assessments and audits of the SMS shall be conducted at planned intervals to evaluate the level of maturity and conformity.

GR7 Continually Improving Service Management (ACT)

REQUIREMENTS

- GR7.1 Nonconformities and deviations from goals shall be identified and actions shall be taken to prevent them from recurring.
- GR7.2 The service management policy, service management plan and all service management processes shall be subject to continual improvement. Respective improvements shall be identified, evaluated and implemented according to the Continual Service Improvement Management process (see PR14).

Process-specific requirements

PR1 Service Portfolio Management (SPM)

REQUIREMENTS

- PR1.1 A service portfolio shall be maintained. All services shall be specified as part of the service portfolio.
- PR1.2 Proposals for new or changed services shall be evaluated based on predicted demand, required resources and expected benefits.
- PR1.3 Design and transition of new or changed services shall be planned considering timescales for realisation, responsibilities, new or changed technology, communication and service acceptance criteria.
- PR1.4 For each service, the internal and external suppliers involved in delivering the service shall be identified, including, as relevant, federation members. Their contact points, roles and responsibilities shall be determined.

PR2 Service Level Management (SLM)

REQUIREMENTS

- PR2.1 A service catalogue shall be maintained.
- PR2.2 For all services delivered to customers, service level agreements (SLAs) shall be in place and reviewed at planned intervals.
- PR2.3 Service performance shall be evaluated against service targets defined in SLAs.
- PR2.4 For supporting services or service components, underpinning agreements (UAs) and operational level agreements (OLAs) shall be agreed as needed and reviewed at planned intervals.
- PR2.5 Performance of supporting services and service components shall be evaluated against targets defined in UAs and OLAs.

PR3 Service Reporting Management (SRM)

REQUIREMENTS

- PR3.1 Service reports shall be agreed with their recipients. Service reports shall, to the extent needed, contain information on the performance against defined or agreed targets as well as information about significant events and detected nonconformities.
- PR3.2 Agreed service reports shall be specified. The specification of each service report shall include its identity, purpose, audience, frequency, content, format and method of delivery.
- PR3.3 Service reports shall be produced and delivered to their recipients according to specifications.

PR4 Service Availability & Continuity Management (SACM)

REQUIREMENTS

- PR4.1 Service availability and continuity requirements shall be identified and reviewed at planned intervals, taking into consideration SLAs.
- PR4.2 Service availability and continuity risks shall be assessed at planned intervals.
- PR4.3 Appropriate measures shall be taken to reduce the probability and impact of identified availability and continuity risks and meet identified requirements.
- PR4.4 Availability of services and service components shall be monitored.

PR5 Capacity Management (CAPM)

REQUIREMENTS

- PR5.1 Service capacity and performance requirements shall be identified and reviewed at planned intervals, taking into consideration SLAs and predicted demand.
- PR5.2 Current capacity and utilisation shall be identified.
- PR5.3 Future capacity shall be planned to meet identified requirements, considering human, technical and financial resources.
- PR5.4 Performance of services and service components shall be analyzed based on monitoring the degree of capacity utilization and identifying operational warnings and exceptions.

PR6 Information Security Management (ISM)

REQUIREMENTS

- PR6.1 Information security requirements shall be identified and information security policies defined and reviewed at planned intervals.
- PR6.2 Information security risks shall be assessed at planned intervals.
- PR6.3 Physical, technical and organizational information security controls shall be implemented to reduce the probability and impact of identified information security risks and meet identified requirements.
- PR6.4 Information security events and incidents shall be handled in a consistent manner.
- PR6.5 Access control, including provisioning of access rights, shall be carried out in a consistent manner.

PR7 Customer Relationship Management (CRM)

REQUIREMENTS

- PR7.1 Service customers shall be identified.
- PR7.2 For each customer, there shall be a designated contact responsible for managing the relationship with the customer.
- PR7.3 Channels used to communicate with each customer, including mechanisms for service ordering, escalation and complaint shall be established.
- PR7.4 Service reviews with customers shall be conducted at planned intervals.
- PR7.5 Service complaints from customers shall be handled in a consistent manner.
- PR7.6 Customer satisfaction shall be managed.

PR8 Supplier Relationship Management (SUPPM)

REQUIREMENTS

- PR8.1 Internal and external suppliers shall be identified.
- PR8.2 For each supplier, there shall be a designated contact responsible for managing the relationship with the supplier.
- PR8.3 Channels used to communicate with each supplier, including escalation mechanisms, shall be established.
- PR8.4 Suppliers shall be evaluated at planned intervals.

PR9 Incident & Service Request Management (ISRM)

REQUIREMENTS

- PR9.1 All incidents and service requests shall be registered, classified and prioritized in a consistent manner, taking into account service targets from SLAs.
- PR9.2 Incidents shall be resolved and service requests fulfilled, taking into consideration information from SLAs and on known errors, as relevant.
- PR9.3 Functional and hierarchical escalation of incidents and service requests shall be carried out in a consistent manner.
- PR9.4 Customers and users shall be kept informed of the progress of incidents and service requests, as appropriate.
- PR9.5 Closure of incidents and service requests shall be carried out in a consistent manner.
- PR9.6 Major incidents shall be identified based on defined criteria and handled in a consistent manner.

PR10 Problem Management (PM)

REQUIREMENTS

- PR10.1 Problems shall be identified and registered in a consistent manner, based on analysing trends on incidents.
- PR10.2 Problems shall be investigated to identify actions to resolve them or reduce their impact on services.
- PR10.3 If a problem is not permanently resolved, a known error shall be registered together with actions such as effective workarounds and temporary fixes.
- PR10.4 Up-to-date information on known errors and effective workarounds shall be maintained.

PR11 Configuration Management (CONFM)

REQUIREMENTS

- PR11.1 Configuration item (CI) types and relationship types shall be defined.
- PR11.2 The level of detail of configuration information recorded shall be sufficient to support effective control over CIs.
- PR11.3 Each CI and its relationships with other CIs shall be recorded in a configuration management database (CMDB).
- PR11.4 CIs shall be controlled and changes to CIs tracked in the CMDB.
- PR11.5 The information stored in the CMDB shall be verified at planned intervals.

PR12 Change Management (CHM)

REQUIREMENTS

- PR12.1 All changes shall be registered and classified in a consistent manner. Classification shall be based on defined criteria and consider different types of changes, including emergency changes and major changes.
- PR12.2 For each type of change, steps shall be defined for handling them in a consistent manner.
- PR12.3 Changes shall be assessed in a consistent manner, taking into consideration benefits, risks, potential impact, effort and technical feasibility.
- PR12.4 Changes shall be approved in a consistent manner. The required level of approval shall be determined based on defined criteria, including the identification of pre-approved changes.
- PR12.5 Changes shall be subject to a post implementation review as needed, and closed in a consistent manner.
- PR12.6 A schedule of changes shall be maintained. It shall contain details of approved changes and intended deployment dates, which shall be communicated to interested parties.

PR13 Release & Deployment Management (RDM)

REQUIREMENTS

- PR13.1 Release and deployment strategies shall be defined, together with the service components and CIs to which they are applied. Strategies shall be aligned with the frequency and impact of releases as well as the technology supporting deployment.
- PR13.2 Criteria for including approved changes in a release shall be defined, taking into consideration the applicable release and deployment strategy.
- PR13.3 Deployment of releases shall be planned, including acceptance criteria, as needed.
- PR13.4 Releases shall be built, tested and evaluated against acceptance criteria prior to being deployed. The extent of release testing shall be appropriate to the type of release and its potential impact on services and customers.
- PR13.5 Deployment preparation shall consider steps to be taken in case of unsuccessful deployment.
- PR13.6 Deployment activities shall be evaluated for success or failure.

PR14 Continual Service Improvement Management (CSI)
REQUIREMENTS
<ul><li>PR14.1 Opportunities for improvement of the SMS and the services shall be identified and registered, based on service reports as well as results from measurements, assessments and audits of the SMS.</li><li>PR14.2 Opportunities for improvement of the SMS and the services shall be evaluated in a consistent manner, and actions to address them identified.</li><li>PR14.3 The implementation of actions for improvement of the SMS and the services shall be controlled in a consistent manner.</li></ul>

Key Objectives of SMS in FitSM:

- **Structured Framework:** The SMS establishes a structured framework for comprehensively managing IT services. It outlines the necessary components, roles, and processes essential for seamless service delivery.

- **Responsibility Allocation:** Within the SMS, roles and responsibilities are clearly defined and allocated, ensuring that individuals and teams understand their specific functions within the service management ecosystem.

- **Process Documentation:** It meticulously documents all aspects of service management processes, providing a comprehensive reference point for the execution of these processes.

- **Control Mechanism:** The SMS acts as a control mechanism, overseeing and regulating service management activities to ensure that they adhere to defined standards and best practices.
- **Continuous Improvement:** A core tenet of the SMS is its commitment to continuous improvement. It facilitates the ongoing refinement of service management processes and practices, driving towards higher levels of efficiency and service quality.
- **Knowledge Repository:** It serves as a repository of knowledge, housing valuable information, guidelines, and best practices that guide service management activities.

In summary, the SMS in FitSM is not merely a passive framework; it is a dynamic and essential component that underpins the effective and efficient delivery of IT services. By providing structure, clarity, and a commitment to ongoing improvement, the SMS ensures that service management activities remain agile, responsive, and aligned with the organization's objectives and customer needs.

1.2.2. Service Portfolio

Within the FitSM framework, the Service Portfolio takes on a central and strategic role as a comprehensive repository encompassing all services offered by an organization. It serves as a meticulously structured repository that facilitates the systematic management of an organization's service offerings. The FitSM Service Portfolio offers a dynamic and panoramic view, encompassing both the current suite of services and those envisioned for the future. It is an instrumental tool that guides decisions about service offerings, including their introduction, retirement, or enhancement.

Key Objectives of the Service Portfolio in FitSM:

- **Comprehensive Catalog:** The FitSM Service Portfolio serves as a comprehensive catalog, documenting all services provided by the organization. It ensures that every service, both current and planned, is thoroughly documented.

- **Strategic Decision Support:** The Service Portfolio aids in strategic decision-making by providing valuable insights into the composition of the service portfolio. This empowers organizations to make informed choices about introducing new services, retiring outdated ones, or improving existing offerings.

- **Resource Management:** It assists in the judicious allocation of resources by offering a clear view of the services in the pipeline. This ensures that resources are allocated effectively to services that align closely with organizational objectives.

- **Customer-Centric Alignment:** The FitSM Service Portfolio encourages alignment with customer needs, helping organizations tailor their services to meet evolving customer demands and market trends effectively.

- **Risk Mitigation:** By providing a comprehensive overview of the entire service landscape, the Service Portfolio enables organizations to proactively manage risks associated with service delivery, enhancing service stability and resilience.

- **Enhanced Transparency:** It enhances transparency by providing stakeholders with a unified and detailed view of the organization's service offerings. This fosters better communication and understanding among teams and stakeholders.

In summary, the Service Portfolio in FitSM is not a static repository but a dynamic and strategic tool. It empowers organizations to manage their service offerings systematically, make informed decisions about service development and retirement, and ensure that services remain aligned with the organization's objectives and customer needs.

1.2.3. Service Level Management

In the FitSM framework, Service Level Management stands as a pivotal discipline that centers on the meticulous orchestration of services, both existing and those on the horizon, to meet predefined performance standards. This practice encompasses a spectrum of activities, including delineation, mutual consensus, vigilant monitoring, and comprehensive reporting of Service Level Agreements (SLAs). Additionally, it ensures that all Operational Level Agreements (OLAs) and Underpinning Contracts (UCs) are firmly established.

Key Objectives of Service Level Management in FitSM:

- **Performance Assurance:** Service Level Management within FitSM ensures that services, both current and future, are consistently delivered at agreed-upon performance levels. This guarantees that services meet defined quality standards.

- **Agreement Establishment:** It is responsible for the meticulous definition and establishment of SLAs. These agreements are critical in clearly defining service expectations and standards.

- **Monitoring and Vigilance:** Service Level Management involves vigilant monitoring of service performance against established SLAs. It ensures that services continue to meet predefined standards and that any deviations are promptly addressed.

- **Comprehensive Reporting:** It provides a mechanism for comprehensive reporting on service performance. Stakeholders are kept informed about service delivery quality through regular and transparent reporting.

- **Internal Collaboration:** Service Level Management promotes internal collaboration through the establishment and management of OLAs. These agreements define how different internal teams work together to deliver services effectively.

- **Contractual Oversight:** In the realm of external service providers, it ensures that UCs are in place and adhere to agreed terms. This oversight guarantees that third-party services are consistent with organizational objectives.

In summary, Service Level Management in FitSM is a dynamic and strategic practice that ensures services consistently meet predefined performance levels. By defining and maintaining SLAs, monitoring performance, and fostering internal and external collaboration, it plays a pivotal role in guaranteeing that services align with organizational goals and customer expectations.

1.2.4. Continuous Improvement

In the FitSM framework, Continuous Improvement stands as a fundamental pillar that underscores the ongoing enhancement of IT service management practices. This component embodies the principle that services should not remain static but should be subject to regular evaluation and refinement, fostering a culture characterized by proactive responsiveness and adaptability.

Key Objectives of Continuous Improvement in FitSM:

* **Regular Evaluation:** Continuous Improvement within FitSM involves the regular and systematic evaluation of IT service management practices. This encompasses assessing processes, performance, and outcomes.

* **Informed Decision-Making:** The insights derived from continuous improvement efforts serve as a foundation for informed decision-making. By analyzing data and feedback, organizations can make strategic adjustments that align services with evolving needs.

* **Efficiency Enhancement:** FitSM's Continuous Improvement process aims to optimize efficiency by identifying and addressing bottlenecks, redundancies, and inefficiencies within service management practices.

- **Quality Enhancement:** This practice ensures that service quality is continuously elevated. By implementing improvements, organizations can raise the standard of service delivery, thereby enhancing customer satisfaction.

- **Proactive Adaptation:** Continuous Improvement encourages a proactive approach to change. It allows organizations to adapt to emerging trends, technologies, and customer expectations swiftly.

- **Cultural Transformation:** Beyond processes, Continuous Improvement seeks to instill a culture of ongoing learning and innovation. It encourages individuals and teams to embrace change, learn from experiences, and contribute to service enhancement.

Continuous Improvement within FitSM is not merely an occasional exercise but a dynamic and ingrained practice. It empowers organizations to proactively refine their IT service management processes, cultivate adaptability, and drive the ongoing evolution of services. By doing so, organizations can better meet the dynamic needs of customers and remain at the forefront of service excellence.

1.2.5. Incident and Problem Management

Within the FitSM framework, the tandem practices of Incident Management and Problem Management hold pivotal roles in ensuring the uninterrupted delivery of services and the continuous improvement of service quality.

Incident Management: Incident Management within FitSM is dedicated to the prompt resolution of incidents to maintain service continuity and minimize disruptions. This practice focuses on swiftly addressing service disruptions, restoring normal operations, and prioritizing customer satisfaction.

Key Objectives of Incident Management in FitSM:

- **Swift Resolution:** FitSM's Incident Management places a premium on rapid incident resolution to minimize downtime and maintain service availability.

- **Customer-Centric Approach:** It is centered around meeting customer needs and expectations, ensuring that incidents are resolved with a strong focus on customer satisfaction.

- **Efficiency Enhancement:** Through well-defined incident categorization and prioritization, FitSM's Incident Management optimizes response times and resource allocation, enhancing overall efficiency.

- **Incident Documentation:** Incidents are thoroughly documented, providing valuable insights into recurring issues that may require Problem Management intervention.

- **Problem Management:** Problem Management in FitSM complements Incident Management by concentrating on the identification and resolution of underlying root causes of recurring incidents. Its primary aim is to prevent the repetition of incidents in the future, thereby enhancing service stability.

Key Objectives of Problem Management in FitSM:

- **Root Cause Analysis:** FitSM's Problem Management conducts in-depth root cause analyses to identify the underlying issues responsible for incidents.

- **Proactive Solutions:** It focuses on developing proactive solutions to eliminate recurring problems and prevent their impact on service quality.

- **Continuous Improvement:** Problem Management in FitSM is an iterative practice. It assesses the effectiveness of solutions and seeks to refine processes to minimize the recurrence of incidents over time.

In summary, Incident and Problem Management in FitSM work in harmony to ensure that services remain resilient and of high quality. While Incident Management rapidly addresses disruptions to maintain service continuity, Problem Management delves deeper to address root causes and drive continuous improvement. These practices are integral to delivering services that are reliable, efficient, and aligned with customer needs.

1.2.6. Change Management

Change Management within the FitSM framework serves as a fundamental discipline focused on the controlled and standardized management of changes. Its core objective is to minimize the disruption to services while ensuring that these changes effectively meet the dynamic requirements of customers and the organization.

Key Objectives of Change Management in FitSM:

- **Standardized Approach:** FitSM's Change Management adheres to a standardized and well-defined approach for handling changes. This consistency ensures that all changes, regardless of their nature, size, or complexity, are subjected to a structured evaluation and approval process.

- **Impact Minimization:** A primary emphasis of Change Management in FitSM is to mitigate the potential adverse effects of changes on services. This is accomplished by conducting meticulous risk assessments and implementing strategies to minimize service disruptions.

- **Alignment with Customer Needs:** FitSM's Change Management process places customer requirements at its core. It strives to understand and align changes with customer expectations, ensuring that services continuously deliver value and satisfaction.

- **Efficiency Enhancement:** Through streamlined change request processes and the judicious use of automation, Change Management in FitSM enhances process efficiency. This results in reduced implementation times for changes while upholding service quality.
- **Risk Evaluation:** Rigorous risk assessment is integral to FitSM's Change Management. The process thoroughly evaluates the potential impacts of changes on service stability, security, and performance, enabling well-informed decision-making.
- **Communication and Transparency:** Effective communication**Error! Bookmark not defined.** is a cornerstone of FitSM's Change Management. It ensures that all stakeholders are well-informed about changes, their potential impacts, and the underlying rationale. This transparency promotes collaboration and trust within the organization.
- **Continuous Improvement:** Change Management in FitSM is an evolving practice that adapts to changing business and technological landscapes. By analyzing change outcomes and incorporating feedback, organizations refine their change processes for ongoing enhancement.

Change Management in FitSM goes beyond the control of changes; it is a dynamic and strategic practice that enables organizations to respond to evolving customer and business needs with agility and precision. By adhering to standardized processes, managing risks, and prioritizing customer requirements, FitSM's Change Management ensures that IT services remain adaptive, reliable, and consistently aligned with the organization's objectives.

1.2.7. Risk Management

Within the FitSM framework, Risk Management plays a pivotal role in safeguarding the integrity and reliability of IT services. This critical component is dedicated to the systematic identification, comprehensive assessment, and effective control of risks that are inherent to the realm of IT services. The overarching objective is to ensure that these risks are managed proactively and mitigated judiciously to prevent any adverse repercussions on service quality and the seamless delivery of IT services.

Key Objectives of Risk Management:

- **Risk Identification:** Risk Management entails a meticulous process of identifying potential risks within the IT service environment. This includes recognizing vulnerabilities, threats, and factors that could impede service performance or reliability.
- **Risk Assessment:** Once risks are identified, they are subjected to a thorough assessment. This evaluation involves gauging the potential impact of each risk and assessing the likelihood of it

occurring. By quantifying risks, organizations can prioritize their response strategies effectively.

- **Mitigation Strategies:** The core essence of Risk Management is devising and implementing risk mitigation strategies. These strategies are designed to proactively reduce the likelihood of risks materializing and minimize their impact if they do occur.
- **Risk Monitoring:** Continuous vigilance is a hallmark of Risk Management. Organizations regularly monitor the risk landscape, staying attuned to evolving threats and vulnerabilities. This ongoing assessment allows for timely adjustments to risk mitigation strategies.
- **Compliance and Governance:** Risk Management aligns with regulatory requirements and governance standards, ensuring that organizations remain in compliance with relevant laws and regulations. This not only mitigates legal risks but also strengthens the organization's reputation.
- **Contingency Planning:** In addition to proactive risk mitigation, Risk Management involves the development of contingency plans. These plans outline the steps to be taken in the event of risk materialization, enabling a swift and effective response to minimize disruptions.

Risk Management in FitSM is far more than risk avoidance; it is a strategic practice that empowers organizations to confront and navigate the complexities of the IT service landscape with confidence. By identifying, assessing, and proactively mitigating risks, organizations can safeguard service quality, maintain reliability, and foster a culture of resilience in the face of ever-evolving challenges.

1.2.8. Measurement and Reporting

The practice of Measurement and Reporting holds a central role in the realm of service management. It serves as a crucial mechanism for evaluating performance and outcomes, ultimately safeguarding the quality of services. This component underlines the significance of systematically collecting pertinent metrics, subjecting them to insightful analysis, and creating comprehensive reports. These reports, in turn, serve as valuable tools for facilitating informed decision-making and fostering alignment with the overarching objectives of the organization.

Key Objectives of Measurement and Reporting:

- **Performance Assessment:** Measurement and Reporting involve the continuous assessment of service performance. By gathering data on key performance indicators (KPIs), organizations gain visibility into how well their services are meeting established benchmarks.

- **Outcome Evaluation:** Beyond just tracking performance, this practice delves into the evaluation of outcomes. It seeks to understand the impact of services on the organization and its stakeholders, enabling data-driven adjustments and improvements.

- **Data-Driven Decision-Making:** The metrics and insights derived from measurement and reporting provide a solid foundation for decision-making. Leaders and decision-makers can rely on these data-driven insights to make informed choices about resource allocation, process optimization, and strategic direction.

- **Continuous Improvement:** By identifying areas where performance falls short of expectations, Measurement and Reporting play a pivotal role in driving continuous improvement efforts. Organizations can pinpoint weaknesses, implement corrective actions, and track the effectiveness of these improvements over time.

- **Alignment with Organizational Goals:** Effective measurement and reporting ensure that service management practices remain in alignment with the broader goals and objectives of the organization. This alignment ensures that services contribute meaningfully to the organization's mission.

- **Transparency and Accountability:** The generation of comprehensive reports promotes transparency within the organization. It enables stakeholders to understand the state of services, fosters accountability, and encourages collaboration among teams working to enhance service quality.

Measurement and Reporting extend far beyond the collection of data. They form a strategic practice that empowers organizations to gauge their service performance, make well-informed decisions, and steer their services in alignment with overarching organizational objectives. By fostering a culture of data-driven excellence and continuous improvement, this practice becomes an invaluable asset in achieving and maintaining service quality.

1.2.9 Resources and Capacity Management

Resource and Capacity Management plays a pivotal role in optimizing the delivery of services by carefully overseeing the availability and utilization of essential resources, encompassing human, technological, and financial aspects. It is paramount to guarantee that these resources are not only in place but are also effectively harnessed to deliver services with maximum efficiency. Moreover, this management discipline is responsible for forecasting and accommodating the ever-evolving demands placed on services, both in the present and in anticipation of future requirements.

Key Objectives of Resource and Capacity Management:

- **Resource Allocation:** Resource and Capacity Management ensures that the right resources, such as skilled personnel, cutting-edge technology, and financial investments, are allocated to specific tasks and services. This allocation is strategic, aiming to make the most efficient use of available assets.

- **Optimal Utilization:** Efficient utilization of resources is a cornerstone of this discipline. It involves tracking resource usage patterns, identifying underutilized assets, and reallocating them to where they can generate maximum value.

- **Demand Forecasting:** To stay ahead of service demands, Resource and Capacity Management involves forecasting the future resource needs of the organization. This forecasting is critical for proactively scaling resources to meet increasing service demands and ensuring service quality.

- **Cost Management:** Keeping services cost-effective is a core consideration. This entails monitoring financial resources closely, identifying areas where cost savings can be achieved without compromising quality, and aligning spending with organizational goals.

- **Risk Mitigation:** Anticipating and addressing potential resource shortages or bottlenecks is another crucial aspect. By identifying potential risks and developing mitigation strategies, this discipline helps maintain consistent service delivery even in the face of unforeseen challenges.
- **Performance Monitoring:** Continuous monitoring of resource and capacity performance ensures that services run smoothly. By establishing key performance indicators (KPIs) and benchmarks, organizations can evaluate the effectiveness of resource allocation and utilization.

Resource and Capacity Management goes beyond merely ensuring that resources are available. It is a strategic discipline that focuses on optimizing the allocation and utilization of resources to meet the dynamic demands of services effectively. By proactively managing resources, organizations can enhance service quality, control costs, and respond swiftly to changing business needs, ultimately contributing to their overall success.

In conclusion, FitSM provides a comprehensive framework that covers various aspects of service management. Each component plays a crucial role in ensuring that IT services are delivered efficiently and meet the desired quality standards.

1.3 FitSM Roles and Responsibilities

FitSM defines a set of roles and responsibilities to ensure the effective implementation of the SMS and the execution of service management processes. These roles include:

- Service Owner, who has overall accountability for a specific service and who maintains the service definition in the service portfolio.
- Process Owner, who is accountable for a process, defining process goals, monitoring their fulfilment and providing resources.
- Process Manager, who reports to the process owner and is responsible for the operational effectiveness and efficiency of a process.
- Process staff member, who is responsible for performing a specific process activity and escalations of exceptions to the process manager.

By assigning clear roles and responsibilities, FitSM establishes accountability and fosters collaboration among individuals involved in service management. This clarity ensures that each role contributes to the overall success and continuous improvement of service delivery. FitSM acknowledges that specific organizational requirements and workflows may necessitate variations in role definitions.

Hence, it provides flexibility for organizations to adapt and tailor the roles and responsibilities to their unique structures and objectives.

By embracing the principles and utilizing the framework of FitSM, organizations can enhance their service management capabilities. The simplicity, flexibility, cost-effectiveness, and integration aspects of FitSM provide a solid foundation for delivering high-quality services, meeting customer expectations, and driving organizational success. FitSM empowers organizations to optimize their service management practices, adapt to changing circumstances, and continuously improve their service delivery processes. It enables them to navigate the complexities of the modern service landscape while ensuring efficiency, effectiveness, and customer satisfaction.

1.4 Differences between FitSM and ITSM

Throughout this section, we will explore the key differences between FitSM and ITSM in more depth, providing a comprehensive understanding of both methodologies. While both frameworks focus on service management within an organization, they have distinct characteristics that set them apart.

One of the primary differences between FitSM and ITSM lies in their scope of implementation. FitSM is specifically designed for smaller organizations, particularly those in the public sector. It offers a streamlined and simplified approach to service management, making it more accessible and cost-effective for such organizations. FitSM focuses on providing practical guidance that can be easily understood and implemented without overwhelming the organization with unnecessary complexity. This adaptability makes FitSM particularly advantageous for smaller organizations with limited resources and technical expertise, as it enables them to implement efficient service management practices while minimizing bureaucracy.

Contrastingly, ITSM, which stands for Information Technology Service Management, is a more comprehensive framework that can be implemented in organizations of all sizes, including large enterprises. ITSM encompasses a broad range of processes, tools, and technologies to manage IT services effectively. It provides a holistic approach that covers service strategy, design, transition, operation, and continual improvement. The extensive scope of ITSM allows organizations to establish consistent and repeatable processes across different departments and functions, ensuring the effectiveness and efficiency of service management practices.

Another significant difference between FitSM and ITSM is the level of complexity involved. FitSM adopts a more lightweight and straightforward approach to service management. It emphasizes simplicity and minimal bureaucracy while still ensuring effective service delivery. This simplicity is achieved by focusing on the essential service management processes and avoiding unnecessary complexity. FitSM's lightweight nature enables smaller organizations to adopt service management practices without overwhelming their limited resources.

On the other hand, ITSM tends to be more comprehensive and detailed. It incorporates numerous processes, practices, and guidelines that cover various aspects of service management.

This level of complexity is beneficial for larger organizations that require a structured and standardized approach to managing their extensive IT operations. ITSM enables organizations to establish a consistent framework and enforce best practices across departments, increasing efficiency and maintaining service quality.

The focus and objectives of FitSM and ITSM also differ. FitSM places a strong emphasis on aligning service management with the needs and requirements of the organization. It aims to provide value by delivering services that meet the specific goals and objectives of the organization. FitSM recognizes that each organization has unique characteristics and tailors its service management practices accordingly. This flexibility allows organizations to adapt and modify their service management processes without being bound to rigid frameworks.

On the other hand, ITSM focuses more on standardization and best practices. It seeks to establish consistent and repeatable processes across the organization to ensure the efficient and effective delivery of IT services. ITSM provides organizations with a set of well-defined processes and guidelines that have proven to be successful in managing IT services. By following these established best practices, organizations can improve service quality and achieve higher levels of operational efficiency.

Moreover, the implementation and adoption of FitSM and ITSM can vary. FitSM can be implemented as a standalone service management system or as an extension to existing ITSM frameworks. It offers flexibility in terms of integration, allowing organizations to align their service management practices with FitSM principles. FitSM's modular approach enables organizations to implement only those components that are necessary and relevant to their specific needs, avoiding unnecessary overhead.

ITSM, on the other hand, is typically implemented as a comprehensive framework that encompasses various processes, tools, and technologies. The implementation of ITSM often requires significant planning, resource allocation, and change management efforts. ITSM implementations often involve the use of specialized software and IT infrastructure to support the delivery and management of IT services. This comprehensive approach ensures that all aspects of service management are addressed in a structured manner, allowing for effective governing and controlling of IT services.

Lastly, while FitSM and ITSM may use similar terms related to service management, there can be variations in their definitions and interpretations. The terminology used in FitSM is designed to be easily understood and implemented by organizations with limited technical expertise. FitSM provides clear and practical definitions for terms and concepts, allowing organizations to adopt and apply the framework without confusion.

On the other hand, ITSM terminology is more extensive and standardized. It often aligns with industry best practices and frameworks such as ITIL (Information Technology Infrastructure Library). ITSM terminology is widely recognized and used across the IT service management community, ensuring consistency, and facilitating communication between organizations using similar frameworks.

In conclusion, FitSM and ITSM differ in terms of their scope, complexity, focus, implementation, and terminology. FitSM's lightweight and tailored approach makes it suitable for smaller organizations, providing simplified and practical guidance for effective service management. ITSM, on the other hand, offers a comprehensive framework that can be implemented in organizations of all sizes, allowing for structured and standardized service management practices. Understanding these differences will help organizations choose the right framework based on their specific needs, resources, and objectives.

1.5. Benefits of FitSM and ITSM

1.5.1. Enhanced Service Delivery Capabilities

By adopting FitSM and ITSM, organizations can enhance their ability to deliver IT services that meet customer expectations. The framework provides a structured approach to managing services, ensuring consistent and reliable delivery. This leads to increased customer satisfaction and loyalty.

1.5.2. Increased Efficiency and Cost-effectiveness

FitSM and ITSM promote process efficiency, enabling organizations to streamline their IT service management practices. By eliminating redundancies, automating routine tasks, and optimizing resource utilization, organizations can achieve higher efficiency and cost- effectiveness. This, in turn, allows them to allocate resources to more strategic initiatives.

1.5.3. Improved Customer Satisfaction

Aligning IT services with the needs and goals of the business enhances customer satisfaction. FitSM and ITSM help organizations understand and meet customer expectations, leading to improved service quality and customer experience. When IT services are consistently reliable, responsive, and aligned with business requirements, customers feel more confident and satisfied with the overall service delivery.

The frameworks enable organizations to establish robust service governance mechanisms, ensuring that service quality is continuously monitored, measured, and improved. Through the implementation of service level management (SLM), incident management, and problem management processes, organizations are better equipped to resolve service issues promptly, minimize service disruptions, and provide proactive support to their customers. By consistently delivering high-quality services, organizations can foster trust, loyalty, and long-term relationships with their customers.

Furthermore, the importance of customer feedback and continual improvement is emphasized. Organizations are encouraged to gather customer feedback through surveys, interviews, or other means, allowing them to understand customer expectations and areas for improvement. By incorporating customer feedback into their service improvement plans, organizations can address identified pain points, tailor their services to customer needs, and enhance overall customer satisfaction.

1.5.4. Alignment with Business Objectives

FitSM and ITSM ensure that IT services are aligned with the broader objectives of the organization. By establishing a structured approach to service management, organizations can link their IT services to business goals and priorities. This alignment allows IT to contribute effectively to business outcomes, driving innovation and competitive advantage.

Both FitSM and ITSM emphasize harmonizing IT services with the overarching goals of the organization. Yet, they distinguish themselves through unique methods and focal points:

FitSM's Unique Alignment Approach:

- Simplified Framework: FitSM offers a more streamlined framework, making it particularly suitable for organizations that need a straightforward approach to align IT services with business objectives without the intricacies of larger frameworks.
- Focused Integration: FitSM emphasizes the integration of IT services with specific business functions, ensuring a tighter alignment with business goals. This can be especially beneficial for organizations with clear, targeted objectives.
- Rapid Implementation: Given its tailored nature, FitSM can often be implemented more rapidly,

allowing organizations to quickly align their IT services with emerging or shifting business objectives.

ITSM's Comprehensive Alignment Approach:

- Holistic View: ITSM, encompassing a range of frameworks, offers a more holistic view of how IT services can align with business objectives, catering to organizations with diverse and complex needs.
- Strategic Planning: Many ITSM frameworks emphasize long- term strategic planning, ensuring that IT services not only align with current business objectives but also anticipate future goals and challenges.
- Broad Integration: ITSM frameworks often focus on integrating IT services across all facets of the organization, ensuring a comprehensive alignment that supports a wide range of business functions and objectives.

In summary, while both FitSM and ITSM focus on aligning IT services with business objectives, FitSM offers a more streamlined and focused approach, ideal for organizations with specific alignment needs. On the other hand, ITSM provides a broader and more comprehensive strategy, suitable for organizations seeking a wide-ranging alignment across multiple business functions and objectives.

By recognizing the distinct strengths of FitSM and ITSM in the realm of business alignment, organizations can choose the framework that best supports their strategic goals and ensures that IT services effectively contribute to desired business outcomes.

1.5.5. Compliance with Standards and Regulations

FitSM and ITSM provide organizations with a framework to ensure compliance with relevant standards and regulations. By following established processes and best practices, organizations can demonstrate adherence to industry standards in areas such as information security, data privacy, and service quality management. This compliance boosts the organization's reputation, instills trust among stakeholders, and reduces the risk of non-compliance penalties.

Both FitSM and ITSM offer organizations frameworks to ensure compliance with relevant standards and regulations. However, there are distinct nuances in their approaches:

FitSM's Unique Compliance Approach:

- Tailored Framework: FitSM provides a more streamlined and simplified framework, making it easier for smaller organizations or those just starting their ITSM journey to achieve compliance without being overwhelmed.
- Modularity: FitSM's modular approach allows organizations to focus on specific areas of

compliance, ensuring that they can prioritize based on their unique needs and challenges.

- Specific Guidance: FitSM often provides more detailed guidance on certain standards, especially those relevant to smaller IT operations or specific sectors, ensuring a more tailored compliance strategy.

ITSM's Broad Compliance Approach:

- Comprehensive Framework: ITSM, being a broader term, encompasses a range of frameworks and standards, offering a more comprehensive approach to compliance. This can be beneficial for larger organizations with complex IT landscapes.
- Flexibility: Given the variety of frameworks under the ITSM umbrella, organizations have the flexibility to choose a framework (like ITIL, COBIT, etc.) that best aligns with their compliance needs.
- Industry Recognition: Some ITSM frameworks have been around for longer and are more widely recognized in certain industries, providing a perceived higher level of trust and assurance to stakeholders.

In essence, while both FitSM and ITSM aim to ensure compliance, FitSM offers a more tailored and modular approach, making it particularly suitable for organizations looking for a more specific and manageable compliance strategy. In contrast, ITSM provides a broader, more flexible approach, catering to a wide range of compliance needs and organizational complexities.

By understanding the unique strengths of both FitSM and ITSM in the realm of compliance, organizations can make informed decisions on which framework to adopt, ensuring they meet industry standards and regulatory requirements effectively.

1.56. Benefits of Implementing FitSM

Implementing FitSM offers a unique set of advantages tailored for organizations aiming to elevate their IT service management practices. This chapter delves into the distinct benefits exclusive to FitSM, providing a deeper understanding of its significance.

Distinctive Service Delivery Enhancement: FitSM's unique approach ensures organizations refine their service delivery, leading to unparalleled efficiency. It uniquely emphasizes defining and documenting service processes, roles, and responsibilities, setting it apart from other frameworks. This distinct focus ensures standardized and automated tasks, minimizing errors and delays. The special emphasis FitSM places on service catalogs and service level management sets it apart, ensuring transparent, consistent, and top-tier service delivery.

Targeted Cost Efficiency: FitSM's approach to cost reduction is unparalleled. It uniquely encourages organizations to conduct regular service portfolio evaluations, ensuring resources are allocated optimally. Its specific guidance on asset and configuration management ensures that organizations avoid redundant expenses, making FitSM's approach to cost efficiency stand out.

Enhanced Customer Satisfaction: FitSM's commitment to service quality is unmatched. Its unique emphasis on service governance, incident management, and problem management ensures rapid issue resolution and proactive customer support. The special attention FitSM gives to customer feedback and continual improvement is a testament to its dedication to enhancing customer satisfaction.

Adaptive Agility and Flexibility: FitSM stands out with its modular and scalable framework, ensuring unmatched agility in IT service deployment and management. Its unique service-oriented mindset and emphasis on service asset and configuration management make it exceptionally adaptable. The special attention FitSM gives to DevOps principles ensures rapid service delivery, setting it apart from other frameworks.

Robust Risk Management and Compliance: FitSM's approach to risk management is second to none. Its unique focus on comprehensive risk assessments and service continuity management ensures organizations are always prepared. Moreover, its dedication to compliance with relevant standards showcases its commitment to security and trust.

Holistic Organizational Alignment: FitSM's holistic approach to IT service management is unparalleled. Its unique emphasis on service integration and management (SIAM) principles ensures seamless collaboration across departments. The regular service review and improvement meetings it promotes are a testament to its dedication to cross-functional collaboration and alignment.

Dedication to Continuous Improvement: FitSM's commitment to continuous improvement is unmatched. Its unique approach to service improvement plans (SIPs) and the Plan-Do-Check-Act (PDCA) model ensures systematic evaluation and enhancement. The special emphasis it places on knowledge management and the use of KPIs sets it apart, ensuring organizations are always at the forefront of service delivery excellence.

In conclusion, FitSM offers a set of benefits that are uniquely tailored to ensure organizations achieve excellence in IT service management. Its distinctive approach ensures improved service delivery, targeted cost efficiency, superior customer satisfaction, adaptive agility, robust risk management, holistic organizational alignment, and a dedicated culture of continuous improvement. By choosing FitSM, organizations are guaranteed a framework that is uniquely designed to meet and surpass customer expectations in the modern digital era.

1.6. Training and Certification in FitSM and ITSM

1.6.1 Importance of Training and Certification

Proper training of IT staff and relevant stakeholders is crucial to ensure the successful implementation of FitSM and ITSM. Training provides individuals with the knowledge and skills to effectively apply the frameworks in real-world scenarios. It helps build a common understanding of the principles, processes, and roles involved in implementing FitSM and ITSM. Certification programs offer a formal recognition of an individual's competence in FitSM and ITSM, further validating their expertise and enhancing their credibility.

1.6.2 FitSM Training and Certification Programs

FitSM offers training and certification programs to support individuals and organizations in developing the required knowledge and skills for implementing and maintaining effective service management practices. Training programs cover essential topics such as the FitSM principles, process descriptions, roles and responsibilities, and documentation requirements.

Certification validates individuals' understanding and competence in FitSM, providing recognition of their expertise and adding value to their professional development. FitSM's training and certification programs enable organizations to build a skilled and knowledgeable workforce, ensuring the successful implementation and ongoing improvement of service management practices.

1.6.3 ITSM Training and Certification Programs

In addition to FitSM-specific training and certification programs, there are also various other ITSM training and certification options available in the market. These programs cover a wider range of ITSM frameworks, methodologies, and best practices, including ITIL, COBIT (Control Objectives for Information and Related Technologies), and ISO/IEC 20000 (International Organization for Standardization/International Electrotechnical Commission).

1.6.4 Benefits of Training and Certification

Training and certification in FitSM and ITSM offer several benefits to individuals and organizations:

- Improved Implementation: Proper training equips individuals with the knowledge and skills to effectively implement FitSM and ITSM within their organizations. They learn best practices, techniques, and tools to successfully manage IT services, leading to better service delivery and customer satisfaction.
- Enhanced Professional Development: Certification in FitSM and ITSM demonstrates an individual's competence and expertise in service management.

It enhances their professional profile, credibility, and career prospects in the ITSM industry.

- Standardization and Consistency: Training and certification promote standardization and consistency in the implementation of FitSM and ITSM. They ensure that individuals follow established processes, practices, and guidelines, leading to consistent service delivery and improved organizational efficiency.

- Advancement of Organizational Goals: Trained and certified professionals can contribute to the alignment of IT services with the organization's objectives. Their expertise enables them to identify improvement opportunities, optimize processes, and drive innovation, ultimately supporting the organization's success.

- Compliance and Risk Management: Training and certification in FitSM and ITSM provide individuals and organizations with a solid understanding of relevant standards and regulations. They can ensure compliance with industry requirements, minimize risks, and improve overall governance and control of IT services.

Conclusion

FitSM and ITSM play a critical role in managing IT services effectively and efficiently. They provide organizations with a structured framework, processes, and best practices to align IT services with business objectives, enhance service delivery, and ensure customer satisfaction.

Training and certification in FitSM and ITSM are essential to equip individuals with the knowledge and skills required for successful implementation. These initiatives enhance competence, promote standardization, and support organizational goals, ultimately resulting in improved service management and organizational success.

CHAPTER 2

UNDERSTANDING THE CROSSROADS

At a pivotal moment in their journey, organizations embarking on FitSM and ITSM implementation face crucial decisions. The choices made here can profoundly influence the success of the endeavor. To navigate this, a deep understanding of available options, their ramifications, and the specific organizational backdrop is essential.

The initial major decision revolves around selecting the most appropriate ITSM framework. FitSM, recognized for its agility and adaptability, empowers organizations to refine their service management while retaining flexibility. The essence of FitSM is to deliver organizational value through efficient service management, ensuring alignment with business goals. With its minimalistic set of requirements, FitSM offers adaptability tailored to an organization's distinct needs and circumstances, providing structure without the burden of excessive bureaucracy or stringent procedures.

However, other frameworks such as ITIL, COBIT, or ISO 20000 may warrant consideration. ITIL, for instance, is widely recognized and has matured over the years to become a globally accepted standard for IT service management. It offers a rich set of practices and guidance, making it suitable for organizations seeking comprehensive IT service management capabilities.

FitSM and ITIL 4, both being IT Service Management frameworks, share common ground in their guiding principles, yet they also exhibit distinct characteristics in their approach and application. Here's a comparison of how FitSM principles align with ITIL 4 guiding principles:

ITIL 4	FitSM
Focus on Value Emphasizes creating, delivering, and supporting value for customers and other stakeholders.	**Service- and Customer-Orientation** Highlights service- and customer-orientation, which aligns with ITIL's focus on value by ensuring that services are designed and delivered with the customer's needs in mind.
Start Where You Are Advises assessing the current situation and making incremental improvements without unnecessarily overhauling existing services.	**Practicality** Principle of practicality aligns with this by advocating for applying simple, proven guidance and building on existing practices.
Progress Iteratively with Feedback Both frameworks stress the importance of making step-by-step progress and using feedback for continuous improvement.	**Continual Improvement** Emphasis on continual improvement mirrors ITIL 4's principle of progressing iteratively, ensuring that services evolve based on ongoing feedback and results.
Collaborate and Promote Visibility Encourages collaboration among teams and transparency in processes.	**Extendibility** Involves leveraging various sources of knowledge, complements this idea by promoting a collaborative and inclusive approach to service management.
Think and Work Holistically Emphasizes the importance of considering the whole, rather than just focusing on individual elements. When applying this principle, organizations are encouraged to recognize and understand the interdependencies in their service management systems.	While FitSM does not have a direct equivalent, its focus on a comprehensive SMS reflects a holistic view of service management, considering all aspects of service delivery.
Keep It Simple and Practical ITIL 4 suggests focusing on simplicity.	**Practicality and Sufficiency** Emphasis on practicality and sufficiency – doing what is necessary and sufficient for achieving objectives.
Optimize and Automate This principle is about maximizing the efficiency and effectiveness of services and processes by optimizing what's already in place and then looking at what can be automated.	FitSM's focus on efficiency and effectiveness, though not explicitly stated as a principle, is inherent in its approach to designing and implementing service management processes.

FitSM and ITIL 4 share common principles like focusing on customer value, iterative progress, practicality, and continual improvement. However, they may articulate these principles differently and apply them in distinct ways, reflecting their unique perspectives on IT service management.

In our exploration of IT service management frameworks, it's evident that FitSM and ITIL 4 not only share common principles but also complement each other in practical applications.

ITIL 4, with its comprehensive and detailed guidance, can effectively augment FitSM's 14 processes. This synergy allows organizations to leverage the structured approach of FitSM while enriching it with the depth and breadth of ITIL 4's best practices. To illustrate this alignment and how ITIL 4 can enhance FitSM's processes, we present a comparative table. This table maps each of FitSM's processes, categorized by Process Requirements (PR) and General Requirements (GR), against the corresponding elements in ITIL 4.

FitSM	ITIL 4
Service Portfolio Management (PR1)	Portfolio Management
	Project Management
	Strategy Management
Service Level Management (PR2)	Service Level Management
	Service Catalog Management
Service Reporting Management (PR3)	Measurement and Reporting Management
Service Availability and	Availability Management

Continuity Management (PR4)	Service Continuity Management
Capacity Management (PR5)	Capacity and Performance Management
	Monitoring and Event Management
Information Security Management (PR6)	Information Security Management
	Service Request Management
Customer Relationship Management (PR7)	Relationship Management
Supplier Relationship Management (PR8)	Supplier Management
Incident and Service Request Management (PR9)	Incident Management
	Service Request Management
Problem Management (PR10)	Problem Management
Configuration Management (PR11)	Service Configuration Management
	IT Asset Management
Change Management (PR12)	Change Enablement
Release and Deployment Management (PR13)	Release Management
	Service Validation and

	Testing
	Deployment Management
Continual Service Improvement Management (PR14)	Continual Improvement
Top Management Commitment & Responsibility (GR1)	Direct, Plan and Improve
Documentation (GR2)	Knowledge Management
Defining the scope of the SMS (GR3)	Direct, Plan and Improve
Planning Service Management (Plan) (GR4)	Direct, Plan and Improve
	Create, Deliver and Support
Implementing Service Management (Do) (GR5)	Create, Deliver and Support
Monitoring and Reviewing Service Management (Check) (GR6)	Drive Shareholder Value
Continually Improving Service Management (Act) (GR7)	Drive Shareholder Value
	Continual Improvement

COBIT, on the other hand, provides a broader focus on governance and control over IT processes and aligns well with organizations that prioritize risk management. ISO 20000, an international standard for IT service management, can offer organizations a recognized benchmark to assess their ITSM practices against industry best practices.

Evaluating each framework requires an in-depth analysis of the organization's objectives, resources, and industry norms. Additionally, considering the organization's maturity level in terms of service management practices and its capacity to implement and sustain the chosen framework is vital. A FitSM and ITSM implementation partner or consultant can provide valuable insights during this evaluation process, helping assess the strengths and weaknesses of each framework option.

Another critical crossroad emerges when deciding whether to outsource IT services or retain them in-house. Outsourcing can yield cost savings and access to specialized expertise, particularly in areas like infrastructure management, software development, or cybersecurity. Moreover, organizations can benefit from the service provider's economies of scale and broader industry knowledge. However, outsourcing also brings complexities and risks, such as potential loss of control, compromised data security, and dependency on third-party vendors. Organizations must carefully evaluate the strategic importance of IT services, the availability of competent service providers, and the required level of integration with other business processes. This decision requires a holistic approach that includes a thorough examination of cost models, risks, service-level agreements, and the overall impact on the organization's operations and goals.

Despite the potential benefits of outsourcing, many organizations opt to keep their IT services in-house. This choice provides them with greater control over operations, data, and service delivery. Organizations that have significant regulatory or compliance requirements may find it more beneficial to retain control over sensitive data and critical operations.

Keeping services in-house also allows organizations to build internal expertise and knowledge. However, this often requires substantial investments in infrastructure, talent acquisition, and ongoing training. It is important to carefully assess the organization's capabilities, budget, and long-term goals to make an informed decision regarding insourcing.

Once the choice regarding ITSM framework and outsourcing has been made, another crossroad involves prioritization. Continuous improvement, a cornerstone of FitSM and ITSM, necessitates organizations to identify areas that require immediate attention while considering resource availability and potential impacts on service delivery. This entails a comprehensive analysis of the current state of service performance, customer feedback, and critical business objectives. Prioritization allows organizations to allocate resources efficiently, ensuring that improvements bring the most significant value and impact to the organization. A systematic approach, such as conducting a service portfolio analysis, can aid in identifying critical services and assessing their alignment with business objectives.

The level of organizational change required often becomes a significant crossroad to navigate during the implementation journey. FitSM and ITSM frameworks necessitate alterations in processes, roles, and organizational culture. Embracing change can be met with resistance and anxiety from employees who are accustomed to their current ways of operating. Sensitivity towards this challenge is crucial, and effective change management strategies must be employed to garner support, cooperation, and ultimately, successful adoption of FitSM and ITSM practices. Leadership support, clear communication, training programs, and involvement of key stakeholders are critical success factors for managing organizational change.

Sustainability and scalability represent another crucial crossroad for organizations. FitSM and ITSM must be implemented with an eye toward the future, considering the organization's growth, evolving technology landscape, and changing customer expectations. It is crucial to anticipate future requirements and incorporate flexibility and adaptability into the implementation strategy. A forward-thinking approach ensures that FitSM and ITSM practices remain relevant and valuable over the long term, supporting the organization's objectives and maintaining a competitive edge. Regular reviews and assessments are essential to identify opportunities for improvement, refine processes, and ensure ongoing alignment with organizational goals.

By proactively exploring, analyzing, and understanding these crossroads, organizations can make informed decisions about their FitSM and ITSM implementation. The ability to navigate these critical junctures guarantees that the chosen path aligns with the organization's objectives, maximizes efficiency, and delivers tangible results. It is at these crossroads that organizations can pave the way for successful FitSM and ITSM implementation, ultimately achieving enhanced service management and driving organizational success.

Conclusion

The journey of implementing FitSM and ITSM is a multifaceted process fraught with pivotal decisions at various crossroads. The strategic choices made, whether concerning the selection of the right framework, the decision to outsource or insource, or the manner of prioritization, can either propel an organization forward or present unforeseen challenges. The overarching key is for organizations to remain attuned to their unique requirements, constantly evolving landscapes, and the essence of service management. By ensuring that every decision is rooted in thorough analysis, a clear understanding of objectives, and foresight, organizations can successfully harness the potential of FitSM and ITSM to foster efficiency, adaptability, and growth.

CHAPTER 3
CHALLENGES IN FITSM AND ITSM
IMPLEMENTATION

I mplementing any new framework or methodology can pose various challenges, and FitSM and ITSM are no exceptions. In this chapter, we will explore some of the common pitfalls and challenges that organizations may encounter during the implementation of FitSM and ITSM and provide in-depth insights on how to overcome them.

3.1 Lack of Leadership Support:

One of the significant challenges in implementing FitSM and ITSM is the lack of support from top-level management. When leaders are not fully committed to the initiative, it becomes challenging to secure necessary resources, allocate budgets, and drive organizational change. Without strong leadership support, it becomes difficult to gain buy-in from employees and establish a culture of continuous improvement. To overcome this challenge, it is crucial to engage executives early on, highlighting the benefits of FitSM and ITSM in terms of cost savings, improved service quality, and increased customer satisfaction. Executives should actively participate in the implementation process, providing clear guidance, and serving as champions for the initiative.

3.2 Resistance to Change:

Introducing FitSM and ITSM often requires significant changes in processes, roles, and responsibilities within an organization. This can lead to resistance from employees who may be accustomed to traditional ways of working. People may feel threatened by the changes, fearing job losses or disruptions to established routines and practices. To mitigate this challenge, organizations must emphasize the need for change, communicate the rationale behind the implementation of FitSM and ITSM, and involve employees in the process. Education and awareness programs can help employees understand the benefits of the framework and dispel any misconceptions or concerns.

Additionally, organizations should provide adequate training and support to employees during the transition phase. This includes offering workshops, seminars, and training sessions that focus on new processes and procedures, as well as providing resources like job aids and documentation to assist employees in adapting to the changes. By addressing the concerns and providing the necessary support, organizations can help employees overcome their resistance and embrace the changes brought about by FitSM and ITSM implementation.

3.3 Inadequate Training and Awareness:

Without proper training and awareness, employees may struggle to understand the principles and practices of FitSM and ITSM. This can result in inconsistent implementation and a lack of understanding of how the framework aligns with organizational goals. To address this challenge, organizations should invest in comprehensive training programs, tailored to different levels and functions within the organization.

Training programs should not only cover the basics of FitSM and ITSM but also provide hands-on learning opportunities and practical guidance on implementing the framework. This could include scenario-based exercises, case studies, and real-world examples to help employees better understand how to apply the principles in their daily work. Regular communication and awareness campaigns can also help to reinforce the principles and build a shared understanding among employees.

Additionally, organizations can establish a knowledge-sharing platform or a community of practice where employees can access resources, ask questions, and share their experiences with FitSM and ITSM. This fosters a culture of continuous learning and ensures that employees have ongoing support as they navigate the challenges and complexities of the framework.

3.4 Lack of Defined Processes and Documentation:

FitSM and ITSM rely on well-defined processes and documented procedures. However, many organizations struggle to develop and maintain these processes and documentation. This can lead to confusion, inefficiencies, and inconsistencies in the implementation of FitSM and ITSM. It is crucial to invest time and effort in establishing clear processes, documenting them adequately, and regularly reviewing and updating them as needed.

To address this challenge, organizations can leverage process mapping techniques, such as BPMN (Business Process Model and Notation), to visualize and standardize their processes. Engaging process owners and stakeholders in the documentation process ensures that the processes reflect the reality of the organization's workflows and requirements. Regular audits and assessments can ensure adherence to the defined processes and help identify areas for improvement.

Organizations should also consider implementing a robust configuration management system to manage and control process documentation. This system should include version control mechanisms, approval workflows, and a centralized repository for easy access and retrieval. Regular reviews of the documented processes should be conducted to validate their accuracy, relevance, and alignment with the organization's evolving needs.

3.5 Limited Communication and Collaboration:

Communication and collaboration are essential for successful FitSM and ITSM implementation. However, organizations often face challenges in fostering effective communication channels and promoting collaboration across teams and departments. Silos and departmental rivalries can hinder the sharing of knowledge and best practices.

To overcome this challenge, organizations should establish clear channels for communication, such as regular team meetings, collaborative platforms, and knowledge- sharing sessions. Cross-functional teams and joint projects can help break down silos and promote collaboration among different departments. Clear roles and responsibilities should be defined to ensure accountability, and regular communication forums should be established to share updates, progress, and lessons learned.

Additionally, leadership should encourage a culture of open communication and provide incentives for collaboration and knowledge sharing. Recognition programs, rewards, and team- building activities can foster a sense of camaraderie and encourage employees to collaborate and share their expertise. By breaking down communication barriers and promoting collaboration, organizations can leverage the collective knowledge and experience of their employees, leading to more effective implementation of FitSM and ITSM.

3.6 Unrealistic Expectations:

Some organizations may have unrealistic expectations about the benefits and outcomes of implementing FitSM and ITSM. It is essential to set realistic goals and expectations and align them with the organization's strategic objectives. Failure to manage expectations can result in disappointment, lack of motivation, and potential abandonment of the framework.

To address this challenge, organizations should conduct a thorough analysis of their current state, identifying areas of improvement and potential challenges. This analysis should serve as the foundation to define clear and measurable objectives for the implementation of FitSM and ITSM. These objectives should be communicated to all stakeholders, ensuring that everyone has a shared understanding of what is achievable and the expected timeframe for achieving the goals.

Regular monitoring and evaluation of progress are crucial to keep expectations in check and make necessary adjustments along the way. Key performance indicators (KPIs) should be established to measure the effectiveness of processes and track the organization's progress. By regularly reviewing these KPIs and communicating the progress to stakeholders, organizations can manage expectations, demonstrate the benefits of FitSM and ITSM, and maintain the momentum for continuous improvement.

3.7 Lack of Continuous Improvement:

FitSM and ITSM emphasize the importance of continuous improvement. However, organizations often struggle to sustain these efforts in the long term. It is essential to establish mechanisms for continuous monitoring, evaluation, and improvement of processes and practices.

Regular reviews of processes and practices should be conducted, focusing on identifying areas for improvement and implementing corrective actions. Organizations can use techniques like gap analysis, root cause analysis, and benchmarking to identify potential improvements and best practices. Employees at all levels should be encouraged to participate in process improvement initiatives by providing feedback, suggesting ideas, and working together to implement changes.

Establishing a continuous improvement culture requires leadership commitment and the active involvement of all employees. Organizations should create platforms for knowledge sharing and encourage employees to share their insights and lessons learned. This can be done through communities of practice, innovation programs, or dedicated improvement projects. Recognizing and rewarding employees for their contributions to continuous improvement efforts further reinforces the culture of ongoing learning and advancement.

Conclusion

Implementing FitSM and ITSM can be a transformative journey for organizations, but it is not without its challenges. It is crucial for organizations to be aware of these pitfalls and have strategies in place to overcome them. By addressing common challenges such as lack of leadership support, resistance to change, inadequate training and awareness, lack of defined processes and documentation, limited communication and collaboration, unrealistic expectations, and lack of continuous improvement, organizations can increase their chances of successful FitSM and ITSM implementation.

Leadership support is crucial in driving the implementation process and ensuring that the necessary resources and budgets are allocated. By engaging executives early on and highlighting the benefits of FitSM and ITSM, organizations can gain buy-in and establish a culture of continuous improvement from the top down. Resistance to change can be mitigated by emphasizing the need for change, communicating the rationale behind the implementation, and involving employees in the process. Providing adequate training and support during the transition phase can also help employees overcome their resistance.

Inadequate training and awareness can lead to inconsistent implementation and a lack of understanding of how FitSM and ITSM align with organizational goals. Organizations should invest in comprehensive training programs tailored to different levels and functions within the organization. Regular communication and awareness campaigns can also help reinforce the principles and build a shared understanding among employees.

Lack of defined processes and documentation can result in confusion and inefficiencies. Organizations should invest time and effort in developing and maintaining clear processes and regularly reviewing and updating them as needed. Process mapping techniques can be used to visualize and standardize workflows, and a robust configuration management system should be implemented to manage and control process documentation.

Limited communication and collaboration can hinder the sharing of knowledge and best practices. Establishing clear channels for communication, promoting cross-functional teams and joint projects, and encouraging a culture of open communication can help break down silos and foster collaboration. Leadership should provide incentives for collaboration and knowledge sharing to further encourage employees to work together.

Unrealistic expectations can lead to disappointment and lack of motivation. It is crucial to set realistic goals and objectives and align them with the organization's strategic objectives. Regular monitoring and evaluation of progress, as well as communication of achievements, can help manage expectations and demonstrate the benefits of FitSM and ITSM.

Lastly, organizations must prioritize continuous improvement to sustain the benefits of FitSM and ITSM in the long term. Regular reviews of processes and practices, employee involvement in improvement initiatives, and a continuous improvement culture fostered by leadership commitment and recognition of employee contributions are essential for ongoing success.

By being aware of these challenges and implementing strategies to overcome them, organizations can increase their chances of successful FitSM and ITSM implementation. This will ultimately lead to improved service quality, increased customer satisfaction, and cost savings for the organization.

CHAPTER 4

GETTING STARTED WITH FITSM: A STEP-BY-STEP GUIDE

n this chapter, we will explore the step-by-step process of getting started with FitSM and implementing it successfully in your organization. FitSM, also known as Lightweight IT Service Management Standard, is an IT service management framework designed to be simple, practical, and cost-effective. By following this guide, you will be able to lay a solid foundation for FitSM implementation and ensure its seamless integration within your organization.

Step 1: Understand FitSM Principles and Objectives

The first step in getting started with FitSM is to familiarize yourself with its principles and objectives. FitSM emphasizes the importance of efficiency, effectiveness, and simplicity in IT service management. It aims to provide a lightweight framework that is easy to understand and implement, without sacrificing the necessary controls and processes.

Adaptable and Scalable Nature of FitSM:

FitSM's design is inherently adaptable, allowing it to be tailored to the specific needs and size of any organization. This flexibility is crucial for businesses ranging from small startups to large enterprises, as it provides a framework that can grow and evolve with the organization.

For Small and Medium-Sized Enterprises (SMEs): FitSM's lightweight nature makes it particularly suitable for SMEs. These organizations can benefit from a structured approach to IT service management without the overhead and complexity often associated with more extensive frameworks.

For Larger Organizations: Larger enterprises can also utilize FitSM, scaling its principles and practices to fit more complex environments and diverse IT service portfolios. The framework's adaptability ensures that it remains relevant and effective even as organizational needs change and grow.

Detailed Exploration of FitSM Principles:

Efficiency in Service Delivery:

- Process Optimization: FitSM encourages the streamlining of service delivery processes. This means identifying and eliminating redundant steps, automating tasks where possible, and optimizing workflows for better efficiency.

- Resource Utilization: Efficient use of resources, including personnel, technology, and budget, is a key focus. FitSM helps organizations to allocate their resources more effectively, ensuring maximum value from investments.
- Reducing Waste: By adopting lean principles, FitSM aids in minimizing waste in service delivery, such as time delays, underutilized resources, and unnecessary expenditures.
- Improving Response Times: Quick and effective response to service requests and issues is a priority. FitSM frameworks help in setting up processes that reduce response and resolution times, enhancing customer satisfaction.

Effectiveness in Meeting User Needs:

- Understanding User Requirements: FitSM stresses the importance of comprehensively understanding what users need from IT services. This involves regular communication with users and stakeholders to ensure their needs are met.
- Setting Clear SLAs: Establishing clear and achievable service level agreements is crucial. These SLAs serve as a formal agreement on the expected level of service, helping to align

expectations between the service provider and the users.

- Alignment with Business Objectives: FitSM ensures that IT services are not just technically sound but also align with the broader business goals of the organization. This alignment is critical for the overall success of the business.

Simplicity in Design and Operation:

- User-Friendly Framework: The simplicity of FitSM makes it accessible and easy to understand, encouraging wider adoption within the organization.
- Ease of Implementation and Maintenance: The straightforward nature of the framework simplifies implementation and ongoing maintenance, reducing the need for extensive training or specialized knowledge.

Objectives of FitSM:

Providing a Lightweight Framework: FitSM offers a practical and less complex alternative, especially beneficial for organizations that find other frameworks too cumbersome or resource intensive.

- Ensuring Necessary Controls and Processes: Despite its simplicity, FitSM maintains a focus on essential controls and processes, ensuring a balanced and effective approach to service management.

- Facilitating Continuous Improvement: The framework encourages a culture of ongoing improvement, where processes and services are regularly evaluated and enhanced. This iterative approach ensures that the IT services remain efficient, effective, and aligned with changing business needs.

In summary, FitSM's adaptable, scalable, and straightforward approach makes it an ideal framework for organizations seeking to implement effective IT service management practices without the complexity and overhead often associated with more extensive frameworks.

Ways to Deepen Understanding of FitSM:

- Comprehensive Study of FitSM Documentation: Delve into the FitSM manuals and guides. These documents provide detailed insights into each aspect of the framework, from service planning and delivery to relationship management and resolution processes.
- Participation in Training and Workshops: Engage in formal training programs or workshops. These sessions, often led by experienced FitSM practitioners, provide practical knowledge and real-world applications of the framework.

- Networking with FitSM Community: Joining a community of FitSM users can be invaluable. Participating in forums, online groups, or local meetups can provide opportunities to learn from others' experiences and challenges.
- Case Studies and Real-world Examples: Review case studies or success stories of organizations that have implemented FitSM. This can provide a clearer picture of how the framework functions in different environments and sectors.
- Interactive Learning Tools: Utilize interactive tools such as webinars, e-learning modules, and simulation exercises. These tools can offer a more engaging way to understand the practical application of FitSM principles.

By thoroughly understanding the principles and objectives of FitSM and engaging in various learning methods, you can effectively apply this framework to enhance your organization's IT service management practices.

Step 2: Assess Your Current IT Service Management Practices

Before you begin implementing FitSM, it is essential to assess your organization's current IT service management practices. This assessment will help you identify areas that need improvement and determine how FitSM can be tailored to meet your specific needs.

Consider conducting a thorough review of your existing ITSM processes, documentation, and tools to identify any gaps or areas requiring enhancement.

To conduct an effective assessment, involve key stakeholders from various departments within your organization. This collaborative approach ensures a comprehensive evaluation of the current state of IT service management. Utilize surveys, interviews, and workshops to gather feedback and insights from employees at different levels. Analyze the collected data to identify patterns, recurring issues, and potential improvement areas.

Conducting a Comprehensive ITSM Assessment:

Review of Existing ITSM Processes:

- Process Mapping: Start by mapping out all existing ITSM processes. This includes incident management, request fulfillment, change management, and others. Understand how these processes are currently executed and managed.
- Efficiency Analysis: Evaluate the efficiency of these processes. Look for delays, bottlenecks, or redundancies that could be streamlined.

Documentation Review:

- Current Policies and Procedures: Examine all existing ITSM-related documentation. This includes service level agreements (SLAs), operating level agreements (OLAs), and any process documentation.
- Compliance and Standards: Check if current practices are in line with industry standards and regulatory requirements. This will help in understanding the gaps in compliance and standard practices.

Tool and Technology Evaluation:

- Existing ITSM Tools: Assess the tools and technologies currently in use for managing IT services. Determine if they are adequate, need upgrades, or should be replaced.
- Integration and Automation: Look for opportunities where automation can improve efficiency. Assess if current tools are well-integrated to provide seamless service management.

Involving Key Stakeholders:

Cross-Departmental Involvement:

- Representation from Various Departments: Ensure that the assessment team includes representatives from all departments that interact with IT services.

This could include IT, customer service, HR, and finance.

- Role of Leadership: Engage organizational leaders to understand strategic objectives and how ITSM can align with these goals.

Gathering Feedback:

- Surveys and Interviews: Conduct surveys and interviews with employees at various levels to understand their perspective on the current ITSM practices.
- Focus Groups and Workshops: Organize focus groups or workshops to discuss specific ITSM areas. This can be an effective way to gather detailed feedback and encourage collaborative problem-solving.

Analyzing Data and Identifying Improvement Areas:

Data Analysis:

- Identifying Patterns and Trends: Analyze the feedback and data collected to identify common issues, patterns, and trends.
- Benchmarking: Compare your current practices against industry benchmarks or best practices to identify areas of improvement.

Identifying Improvement Areas:

- Prioritizing Issues: Based on the analysis, prioritize the issues that need immediate attention.
- Alignment with Business Goals: Ensure that the identified improvement areas align with the overall business objectives and strategies.

Reporting and Planning:

- Creating a Comprehensive Report: Compile the findings into a detailed report that outlines the current state of ITSM practices, identified gaps, and potential areas for improvement.
- Action Plan Development: Develop an action plan that outlines the steps needed to address the identified gaps and areas for improvement. This plan should include timelines, responsibilities, and resource requirements.

Preparing for FitSM Implementation:

Alignment with FitSM Principles:

- Mapping to FitSM: Map the identified improvement areas to specific FitSM principles and processes. This will help in tailoring the FitSM framework to your organization's specific needs.

Setting the Stage for Change:

- Change Management Strategy: Develop a change management strategy to ensure a smooth transition to FitSM practices.
- Stakeholder Engagement: Continuously engage with stakeholders throughout the process to ensure buy-in and support for the upcoming changes.

By conducting a thorough assessment of your current ITSM practices and involving key stakeholders in the process, you can create a solid foundation for successfully implementing the FitSM framework. This approach ensures that the transition to FitSM is well-informed, strategic, and aligned with your organization's specific needs and objectives.

Step 3: Defne Your Implementation Goals and Scope

Once you have assessed your current ITSM practices, it is crucial to define your specific objectives for adopting FitSM and the implementation goals and scope. Determine what you want to achieve with FitSM and identify the specific areas of IT service management that you plan to address. Clearly defining your goals and scope will help you stay focused and ensure that your FitSM implementation remains aligned with your organization's objectives. Consider the aspects of your IT service management practices that need improvement or streamlining, such as incident management, change management, service level agreements, or service catalog management. Clearly articulating your objectives will guide the entire implementation process and help you measure the success of the initiative. Additionally, establish key performance indicators (KPIs) aligned with your objectives to monitor progress and evaluate the impact of FitSM implementation.

When defining your implementation goals, consider both short-term and long-term objectives. Short-term goals could include improving incident management processes, enhancing the availability of services, or streamlining change management. Long-term goals may involve achieving ISO/IEC 20000 certification, establishing a service catalog, or implementing a service improvement program. By clearly defining your goals and scope, you will have a roadmap to follow, and a clear vision of what success looks like.

Setting Clear Implementation Goals:

Short-Term Goals:

- Immediate Process Improvements: Identify specific ITSM processes that require immediate attention. This could include enhancing incident response times, improving the efficiency of service requests, or streamlining the change management process.

- Quick Wins: Focus on goals that can be achieved relatively quickly and can demonstrate the benefits of FitSM to stakeholders. For example, reducing the backlog of unresolved IT issues or improving user satisfaction scores.

Long-Term Goals:

- Strategic Alignment: Ensure that your long-term goals align with the overall strategic objectives of your organization. This could involve integrating IT services with business processes more effectively or supporting business growth through scalable IT services.
- Compliance and Certification: If relevant, set a goal to achieve compliance with standards like ISO/IEC 20000, which demonstrates a commitment to high-quality IT service management.
- Continuous Service Improvement: Establish goals for ongoing improvement in IT service quality and efficiency, such as implementing a continuous service improvement program or adopting new technologies to enhance service delivery.

Defining the Scope of Implementation:

Areas of Focus:

- Specific ITSM Processes: Determine which areas of IT service management you want to address with

FitSM. This could include incident management, problem management, change management, service level management, or any other area that needs improvement.

- Service Catalog Management: Consider whether developing or refining your service catalog is a priority. A well-defined service catalog can improve clarity around service offerings and expectations.

Organizational Coverage:

- Phased Rollout: Decide if you will implement FitSM across the entire organization at once or start with specific departments or services. A phased approach can help manage the change more effectively.
- Integration with Existing Practices: Determine how FitSM will integrate with existing ITSM practices and tools. This includes assessing the need for changes or upgrades to current ITSM software and tools.

Establishing Key Performance Indicators (KPIs):

Alignment with Goals:

- Relevant KPIs: Choose KPIs that directly reflect progress towards your defined goals. For example, if improving incident management is a goal, relevant KPIs might include mean time to resolve incidents or user satisfaction ratings.

- Measurable and Achievable: Ensure that KPIs are quantifiable and achievable within the set timelines. This helps in accurately measuring progress and identifying areas needing further improvement.

Monitoring and Evaluation:

- Regular Reviews: Set up a schedule for regular reviews of KPIs to monitor progress. This could be monthly, quarterly, or at another interval that makes sense for your organization.
- Adjustments and Adaptations: Be prepared to adjust goals and KPIs as you progress with the implementation. Flexibility is key to adapting to challenges and changes in organizational priorities.

Creating a Roadmap for Success:

Implementation Plan:

- Detailed Action Plan: Develop a detailed plan that outlines the steps, timelines, and resources required to achieve your goals. This plan should include specific tasks, responsible parties, and milestones.
- Risk Management: Identify potential risks and challenges in the implementation process and develop strategies to mitigate them.

Vision of Success:

- Clear End Goals: Define what success looks like for each goal. This clarity will help keep the team focused and motivated.
- Communication of Vision: Share the vision and roadmap with all stakeholders to ensure alignment and buy-in across the organization.

By clearly defining your goals, scope, KPIs, and creating a detailed implementation roadmap, you set a solid foundation for a successful FitSM implementation. This structured approach ensures that the initiative is aligned with your organization's objectives and is measurable, manageable, and adaptable to changing needs.

Step 4: Establish a Project Team and Roles

FitSM should not be implemented in isolation. It requires collaboration and involvement from various stakeholders within your organization. Establish a project team consisting of individuals from different departments who will be responsible for the implementation.

Defne their roles and responsibilities, ensuring that the team represents a cross-section of the organization and has the necessary expertise to drive the initiative forward.

Forming a Diverse Project Team:

Cross-Departmental Representation:

- Inclusive Team Composition: Select team members from various departments such as IT, customer service, HR, and finance. This diversity ensures that multiple perspectives are considered, and the FitSM implementation is aligned with the needs of the entire organization.
- Skillset Variety: Include individuals with a mix of skills, including technical IT knowledge, project management, change management, and communication skills.

Stakeholder Involvement:

- Engaging Key Stakeholders: Identify and involve key stakeholders who can influence or will be affected by the FitSM implementation. Their input and support can be crucial for the success of the project.

Regular Updates and Feedback: Establish a mechanism for regular communication with stakeholders to keep them informed and gather their feedback throughout the project.

Defining Roles and Responsibilities:

Project Leader:

- Overall Coordination: Assign a project leader who will be responsible for overseeing the entire FitSM implementation. This person should have strong leadership skills and a good understanding of IT service management.
- Liaison with Management: The project leader should act as the main point of contact between the project team and higher management, ensuring alignment with organizational goals.

ITSM Specialists:

- Technical Expertise: Include ITSM specialists who have in-depth knowledge of IT service management processes and FitSM framework specifics.
- Process Design and Implementation: These team members will be crucial in designing and implementing the FitSM processes within the organization.

Change Management Lead:

- Facilitating Change: Appoint a change management lead to handle the human aspect of the implementation, including addressing resistance, communicating changes, and ensuring smooth adoption of new processes.

- Training and Support: Responsible for organizing training sessions and providing support to employees during the transition.

Communication Officer:

- Internal Communication: Designate a communication officer to manage all internal communications related to the FitSM implementation. This includes creating awareness, disseminating information, and ensuring clear and consistent messaging.
- Feedback Collection: This role involves gathering feedback from various departments and reporting it back to the project team for continuous improvement.

Quality Assurance and Compliance Officer:

- Monitoring and Evaluation: This role focuses on ensuring that the FitSM implementation adheres to the defined quality standards and meets the set objectives.
- Compliance Checks: Regularly check for compliance with internal policies and external regulations related to IT service management.

Collaborative Approach and Continuous Learning:

Regular Team Meetings:

- Coordination and Progress Tracking: Conduct regular meetings to coordinate activities, track progress, and address any challenges or roadblocks.
- Shared Learning: Use these meetings as an opportunity for team members to share insights, learn from each other, and make collective decisions.

Role Flexibility and Development:

- Adaptive Roles: Encourage team members to be flexible in their roles and take on different responsibilities as needed.
- Professional Development: Provide opportunities for team members to develop their skills and knowledge in areas relevant to FitSM and IT service management.

By establishing a well-rounded project team with clearly defined roles and responsibilities, and fostering a collaborative and adaptive environment, your organization can effectively implement the FitSM framework. This approach ensures that the implementation is comprehensive, aligned with organizational goals, and adaptable to evolving needs and challenges.

Step 5: Engage Stakeholders

Engaging all relevant stakeholders is essential for a smooth and successful FitSM implementation. This includes top management, IT staff, service providers, and any department or individual that will be impacted by the changes. Effective communication and collaboration are key to gaining their buy-in and support. Clearly explain the benefits of FitSM, such as improved service quality, increased efficiency, enhanced customer satisfaction, and cost savings. Encourage active involvement from stakeholders throughout the implementation process to ensure alignment with organizational goals and to address any concerns or resistance.

Identifying and Understanding Stakeholders:

Stakeholder Mapping:

- Comprehensive Identification: Begin by identifying all potential stakeholders who will be affected by or have an influence on the FitSM implementation. This includes top management, IT staff, service providers, end-users, and other departmental staff.
- Understanding Stakeholder Needs: Understand the needs, expectations, and concerns of different stakeholders. Recognize that different groups may have varied interests and priorities regarding IT service management.

Stakeholder Analysis:

- Assessing Influence and Interest: Analyze the level of influence and interest of each stakeholder group. This will help in determining the approach for engagement and communication.
- Categorization: Categorize stakeholders based on their role and level of impact on the project. This helps in tailoring communication and engagement strategies.

Effective Communication Strategies:

Clear and Consistent Messaging:

- Benefits of FitSM: Communicate the benefits of FitSM clearly, such as improved service quality, increased efficiency, enhanced customer satisfaction, and potential cost savings.
- Tailored Communication: Customize the messaging to address the specific interests and concerns of each stakeholder group.

Multiple Communication Channels:

- Diverse Channels: Use a variety of communication channels such as meetings, emails, newsletters, and intranet postings to reach different stakeholders.

- Feedback Mechanisms: Implement channels for stakeholders to provide feedback, ask questions, and express concerns.

Fostering Collaboration and Involvement:

Active Stakeholder Participation:

- Involvement in Decision-Making: Involve stakeholders in key decisions related to FitSM implementation. This could include participation in planning meetings, working groups, or feedback sessions.
- Role in Implementation: Assign specific roles or tasks to stakeholders where appropriate, to encourage ownership and active participation in the implementation process.

Addressing Concerns and Resistance:

- Open Forums for Discussion: Create opportunities for open discussion where stakeholders can voice their concerns or resistance.
- Problem-Solving Approach: Address concerns proactively by working collaboratively with stakeholders to find solutions.

Aligning with Organizational Goals:

Linking FitSM to Business Objectives:

- Strategic Alignment: Demonstrate how FitSM implementation aligns with and supports the broader organizational goals and strategies.
- Showcasing Value: Provide examples or case studies that illustrate the value FitSM can bring to the organization.

Continuous Engagement:

- Regular Updates: Keep stakeholders informed about the progress of the FitSM implementation, including successes and challenges.
- Long-Term Involvement: Ensure that stakeholder engagement is not just a one-time activity but a continuous process throughout the implementation and beyond.

Monitoring and Adjusting Engagement Strategies:

Evaluating Engagement Effectiveness:

- Assessing Impact: Regularly assess the effectiveness of stakeholder engagement strategies. This can be done through surveys, feedback forms, or informal discussions.
- Adapting Strategies: Be prepared to adapt engagement strategies based on feedback and changing needs.

Celebrating Milestones:

- Recognizing Contributions: Acknowledge and celebrate the contributions of stakeholders at various milestones. This helps in maintaining enthusiasm and support for the project.

By engaging stakeholders effectively through clear communication, active involvement, and continuous alignment with organizational goals, you can ensure a smooth and successful FitSM implementation. This approach not only addresses concerns and resistance but also fosters a sense of ownership and commitment among all those involved.

Step 6: Establish a Project Team

The project team should consist of individuals with a mix of technical knowledge, process expertise, and organizational influence. Key roles that should be considered include a project manager, a process owner for each FitSM process, and subject matter experts from various IT service management areas. Clearly define the responsibilities of each team member and communicate them effectively to ensure everyone understands their role in the FitSM implementation.

Composition of the Project Team:

Diverse Skill Set:

- Technical Knowledge: Include team members with strong technical expertise in IT service management systems and tools.
- Process Expertise: Ensure the presence of individuals who have a deep understanding of ITSM processes and best practices.
- Organizational Influence: Involve members who have the authority or influence within the organization to drive changes and facilitate decision-making.

Role Identification:

- Project Manager: Appoint a project manager who will lead the FitSM implementation. This person should have strong project management skills and experience in managing IT projects.
- Process Owners: Assign a process owner for each FitSM process (like incident management, service request management, etc.). These individuals will be responsible for overseeing the implementation and ongoing management of their respective processes.
- Subject Matter Experts (SMEs): Include SMEs from various ITSM areas who can provide in-depth

knowledge and guidance on specific aspects of the implementation.

Defining Roles and Responsibilities:

Clear Role Definitions:

- Documented Responsibilities: Clearly document the responsibilities and expectations for each role. This should include specific tasks, objectives, and deliverables.
- Understanding of Roles: Ensure that each team member understands their role and how it contributes to the overall FitSM implementation.

Alignment with Organizational Structure:

- Integration with Existing Roles: Align the project roles with the existing organizational structure to ensure smooth collaboration and minimize disruption.
- Leveraging Existing Expertise: Utilize the existing expertise within the organization. For example, if there are staff members who have experience with similar implementations or ITSM frameworks, their knowledge can be invaluable.

Communication and Collaboration:

Effective Communication:

- Regular Meetings: Schedule regular team meetings to discuss progress, address challenges, and coordinate activities.
- Open Channels of Communication: Establish open lines of communication among team members to facilitate easy sharing of information and collaboration.

Collaborative Environment:

- Teamwork and Support: Foster a collaborative environment where team members support each other and work together towards common goals.
- Conflict Resolution: Implement mechanisms for resolving conflicts or disagreements within the team constructively.

Monitoring and Support:

Performance Tracking:

- Regular Reviews: Conduct regular reviews of each team member's performance and the progress of their respective areas.
- Feedback and Adjustments: Provide constructive feedback and make adjustments to roles and responsibilities as needed.

Resource Allocation:

- Ensuring Adequate Resources: Ensure that the project team has the necessary resources, including tools, technology, and time, to effectively carry out their roles.
- Training and Development: Provide opportunities for training and professional development, especially in areas critical to the FitSM implementation.

Continuous Improvement:

Learning and Adaptation:

- Lessons Learned: Encourage team members to share lessons learned and best practices from their areas of expertise.
- Adaptation to Change: Be open to adapting team strategies and approaches based on the evolving needs of the project and feedback from team members.

By establishing a well-rounded project team with clearly defined roles, responsibilities, and a collaborative working environment, the FitSM implementation can be effectively managed and executed. This approach ensures that the project leverages diverse skills and expertise, aligns with organizational structures, and is adaptable to changing requirements and challenges.

Step 7: Conduct Gap Analysis

Conducting a comprehensive gap analysis is critical to understanding the current state of your IT service management practices and identifying areas that require improvement or alignment with FitSM principles. This analysis involves thoroughly reviewing existing processes, documentation, tools, and capabilities. Compare these against FitSM requirements and best practices and standards, such as those outlined in ISO/IEC 20000 and ITIL, to identify gaps in your organization's IT service management maturity. This exercise helps establish a clear baseline and provides insights into the specific gaps that need to be bridged.

Review of Current ITSM Practices:

- Existing Processes and Documentation: Thoroughly review your current ITSM processes, documentation, tools, and capabilities. This includes how incidents, service requests, changes, and other ITSM activities are managed.
- ITIL Best Practices: Evaluate your practices against ITIL guidelines. ITIL offers a comprehensive set of best practices covering the entire service lifecycle, which can provide valuable insights into areas like service design, strategy, and continuous improvement.

- Alignment with ISO/IEC 20000 Standards: Compare your current ITSM practices with the requirements of ISO/IEC 20000. This international standard provides a formalized framework for ITSM, focusing on compliance and quality management.
- Certification Goals: If aiming for ISO/IEC 20000 certification, identify the specific gaps that need to be addressed to meet the standard's requirements.

Gap Identification and Prioritization:

- Identifying Discrepancies: Pinpoint where your current ITSM practices do not align with FitSM, ITIL best practices, and ISO/IEC 20000 standards. Look for missing processes, inadequate documentation, or areas needing skill enhancement.
- Risk and Impact Assessment: Assess the risk and impact of these gaps on service delivery and organizational goals. Prioritize the gaps based on their criticality and the resources required to address them.

Developing an Action Plan:

- Actionable Steps: For each identified gap, develop actionable steps to address it. This might include process redesign, adopting new tools, staff training, or policy updates.

- Resource Allocation and Timeline: Determine the resources needed for each action and establish a realistic timeline for implementation.

Monitoring and Continuous Improvement:

- Regular Reviews and Adjustments: Set up regular review meetings to monitor progress in addressing the gaps. Be prepared to make adjustments based on feedback and evolving needs.
- Stakeholder Feedback: Regularly seek feedback from stakeholders to ensure that the changes align with user needs and organizational objectives.

By conducting a gap analysis that considers FitSM principles, ITIL best practices, and ISO/IEC 20000 standards, your organization can establish a clear baseline for ITSM maturity. This comprehensive approach ensures that your ITSM practices are not only aligned with recognized standards but are also continuously improved upon, leading to enhanced service quality and efficiency.

Step 8: Develop an Implementation Plan

To ensure a smooth and successful FitSM implementation, it is crucial to develop a detailed implementation plan. This plan should outline the tasks, timelines, and resources required to achieve your implementation goals. Break the project into manageable phases and allocate necessary resources such as personnel, infrastructure, and budget.

Additionally, consider potential risks and develop strategies to mitigate them. Defne clear roles and responsibilities for each stakeholder involved in the implementation. This plan will act as a roadmap, ensuring that everyone understands their roles, responsibilities, and the overall timeline for implementation, thereby fostering accountability and coordination.

Clearly communicate the plan to all stakeholders involved, ensuring that everyone understands their role and the expected outcomes.

When developing the implementation plan, consider the following factors:

- Timeframe: Determine a realistic timeline for each phase of the implementation. Consider resource availability, dependencies, and the impact on day-to-day operations.
- Resource Allocation: Identify the resources required for each phase, including human resources, budget, and tools. Ensure that the necessary resources are allocated accordingly to support the implementation.
- Dependencies: Identify any dependencies between different processes or departments within your organization. Address these dependencies and establish communication and coordination mechanisms to ensure a smooth implementation.

- Milestones and Deliverables: Defne clear milestones and deliverables for each phase of the implementation. This will help track progress and ensure that the project stays on schedule.

Step 9: Customize and Adapt FitSM to Your Organization

FitSM is designed to be flexible and adaptable, allowing organizations to tailor it to their specific needs. Take the time to customize and adapt FitSM frameworks, processes, and templates to align with your organization's existing practices and culture. This customization ensures that FitSM integrates seamlessly within your IT service management landscape.

Remember to document these adaptations as part of your implementation documentation for future reference.

To customize FitSM effectively, involve your project team and key stakeholders in the process. Review your existing IT service management practices and identify areas where FitSM can complement or enhance them. Work collaboratively to adjust FitSM processes, such as incident management, problem management, and change management, to ft your organization's unique requirements. Consider incorporating existing documentation, policies, and procedures into the FitSM framework to ensure continuity and adoption.

Customizing FitSM to Your Organization's Needs:

Adapting FitSM Frameworks and Processes:

- Incident Management: For instance, if your organization already has a well-established incident management process, you can integrate FitSM's incident management guidelines with your existing procedures. This might involve aligning FitSM's incident categorization and prioritization methods with your current system.

- Problem Management: FitSM's problem management can be tailored to fit into your organization's existing approach to identifying and resolving systemic issues. For example, if your organization uses a specific root cause analysis technique, incorporate this into the FitSM problem management process.

- Change Management: Adapt FitSM's change management process to align with your organization's change approval levels and authorities. If your organization has a Change Advisory Board (CAB), FitSM's change management process can be customized to detail how the CAB fits into the overall change management workflow.

Integrating FitSM with Existing Documentation and Policies:

- Service Level Agreements (SLAs): If your organization already has SLAs in place, review and revise them to ensure they align with FitSM's service level management process. This might include adjusting the metrics and targets in your SLAs to match FitSM's recommendations.
- Operational Level Agreements (OLAs): FitSM's guidelines on OLAs can be integrated with any existing internal agreements you have with other departments to ensure cohesive service delivery.

Ensuring Continuity and Adoption:

- Customized Templates: Use FitSM's templates as a starting point and modify them to include elements from your existing ITSM documentation. This helps in maintaining continuity and eases the transition for staff.
- Cultural Alignment: Adjust FitSM's recommendations to fit your organization's culture. For example, if your organization values a high degree of collaboration, ensure that the adapted FitSM processes encourage and facilitate collaborative efforts across departments.

Documentation and Involvement:

Documenting Adaptations:

- Implementation Documentation: Keep a detailed record of how FitSM has been adapted for your organization. This documentation should include the rationale behind each adaptation and how it aligns with your existing practices.
- Future Reference: Ensure that this documentation is easily accessible for future reference, especially for new team members or during audits.

Collaborative Customization Process:

- Involving the Project Team and Stakeholders: Engage your project team and key stakeholders in the customization process. Their insights and knowledge of existing practices will be invaluable in ensuring that FitSM is adapted effectively.
- Feedback Loops: Establish feedback loops to continuously improve the adapted processes. Regularly review the effectiveness of the customized FitSM framework and make adjustments as needed.

By taking the time to customize and adapt FitSM to your organization's specific needs and existing practices, you ensure a more seamless integration and higher adoption rate. This tailored approach not only respects the unique aspects of your organizational culture but also leverages the strengths of your current ITSM practices, enhancing them with FitSM's structured and best practice-oriented approach.

Step 10: Train and Educate Your Team

To ensure a successful implementation, it is crucial to train and educate your team members about FitSM. Conduct training sessions and workshops to familiarize them with the FitSM framework, its processes, and any customized elements specific to your organization.

Provide additional training for individuals who will fulfill specific roles within FitSM, such as service managers or process owners. This training will equip your team with the necessary knowledge and skills to successfully implement and manage FitSM.

Develop a comprehensive training plan to ensure that all relevant team members receive the required education. Provide both theoretical and practical training sessions, allowing participants to apply their learning to real-life scenarios. Training could include classroom sessions, e-learning modules, hands-on exercises, and simulations. Consider partnering with external experts or consultants to provide specialized training and guidance tailored to FitSM implementation. Regular awareness campaigns, through email, newsletters, or posters, can also help foster a culture of compliance with FitSM principles. Promote continuous learning and knowledge sharing by establishing a central repository of training materials and resources.

Tailoring Training to FitSM Specifics:

Utilizing FitSM Official Training Resources:

- FitSM Training Courses: Direct team members to the official FitSM training courses available on the FitSM website. These courses are specifically designed to cover various aspects of the FitSM framework, from basic principles to advanced topics.
- FitSM Qualifications: Encourage team members to pursue FitSM qualifications, which are structured into different levels – FitSM Foundation, FitSM Advanced, and FitSM Expert. Each level provides a deeper understanding of the framework and its application.

FitSM Workshops and Seminars:

- FitSM Workshops: Organize or enroll team members in FitSM workshops. These workshops are practical and interactive, focusing on the application of FitSM in real-world scenarios.
- Expert-Led Seminars: Invite FitSM experts or certified trainers to conduct seminars that provide insights into the framework's best practices and latest developments.

Integrating FitSM Training with Organizational Practices:

Customized Internal Training Sessions:

- Adapting FitSM Training to Your Organization: Develop internal training sessions that adapt FitSM principles to your organization's specific context. Use case studies and examples from your own ITSM practices to illustrate how FitSM can be applied.
- Role-Specific Training: Tailor training sessions for different roles, such as service managers or process owners, focusing on the aspects of FitSM most relevant to their responsibilities.

Practical Application and Hands-On Learning:

- Simulation Exercises: Implement simulation exercises that mimic real-life ITSM scenarios within your organization. Use these simulations to demonstrate how FitSM processes can be applied and managed.
- FitSM Tools and Templates: Train team members on how to use specific FitSM tools and templates. This can include incident management tools, service catalog templates, or change management documentation aligned with FitSM standards.

Continuous Learning and FitSM Community Engagement:

Ongoing Education and Updates:

- FitSM Webinars and Online Resources: Regularly participate in FitSM webinars and utilize online resources for ongoing education. Encourage team members to stay updated with the latest FitSM developments and practices.
- FitSM Newsletters and Publications: Subscribe to FitSM newsletters and publications to receive regular updates and insights.

Building a FitSM Knowledge Base:

- Internal FitSM Resource Center: Create an internal repository of FitSM resources, including training materials, guidelines, and best practices. Encourage team members to contribute to and utilize this knowledge base.
- FitSM Community Participation: Promote participation in the FitSM community, such as online forums or user groups, where team members can exchange ideas and experiences with other FitSM practitioners.

By leveraging official FitSM training resources, customizing training to align with organizational needs, and promoting continuous learning and community engagement, your team will be well-equipped to implement and manage the FitSM framework effectively. This approach ensures a deep and practical understanding of FitSM, tailored to the unique context of your organization.

Step 11: Implement FitSM Processes and Controls

Strategic Implementation of FitSM Processes:

Prioritizing Key Processes:

- Alignment with Goals: Start by implementing FitSM processes that are most aligned with your organization's specific goals and objectives. For example, if improving incident response is a priority, begin with the incident management process.
- Streamlining for Efficiency: Review each process for potential streamlining opportunities. Remove redundant steps and simplify procedures to enhance efficiency without compromising effectiveness.

Phased Implementation Approach:

- Gradual Rollout: Implement the FitSM processes in phases. This allows your team to adjust to changes gradually and ensures that each process is given the attention it needs for successful implementation.
- Pilot Testing: Consider pilot testing processes in selected departments or teams before a full-scale

rollout. This can help identify potential issues and make necessary adjustments.

Integrating OKRs and KPIs in FitSM Implementation:

Understanding OKRs and KPIs:

- Objectives and Key Results (OKRs):

    o Focus on Goals and Outcomes: OKRs are a goal-setting framework used to define and track objectives and their outcomes. They are typically ambitious and help align and motivate teams with clearly defined goals.

    o Components: An OKR consists of an Objective, which is a clearly defined goal, and Key Results, which are specific measures used to track the achievement of that goal.

- Key Performance Indicators (KPIs):

    o Measuring Performance: KPIs are quantifiable measures used to evaluate the success of an organization, employee, or process in meeting objectives for performance.

    o Operational Focus: Unlike OKRs, KPIs are often more operational and focus on the efficiency and effectiveness of processes.

Using OKRs and KPIs in FitSM Implementation:

Setting FitSM Objectives with OKRs:

- Defining Ambitious Goals:

    o Use OKRs to set ambitious, high-level goals for your FitSM implementation. For example, an Objective could be "To significantly enhance IT service delivery efficiency within 6 months."

    o Key Results for Measurement: Define Key Results that are specific and measurable. For instance, Key Results for the above objective could include "Reduce incident resolution time by 30%" or "Achieve 95% user satisfaction in IT services."

Monitoring Process Performance with KPIs:

- Operational Efficiency: Use KPIs to measure the operational aspects of the FitSM processes. For example, a KPI for incident management could be "Average time to resolve incidents."
- Continuous Improvement: Regularly monitor these KPIs to gauge the effectiveness of the implemented processes and identify areas for improvement.

Aligning OKRs and KPIs:

Alignment for Strategic and Operational Excellence:

- Linking OKRs and KPIs: Ensure that your KPIs are aligned with your OKRs. The KPIs should provide the data needed to measure progress towards achieving your OKRs.
- Balanced Approach: While OKRs push for ambitious improvements, KPIs ensure that day-to-day operations are optimized and aligned with these broader goals.

Communication and Review:

- Regular Reviews: Conduct regular review sessions to assess progress against both OKRs and KPIs. This helps in maintaining alignment and focus.
- Adaptation and Adjustment: Be prepared to adapt your OKRs and KPIs as you progress with the FitSM implementation. As goals are achieved or challenges arise, adjust your OKRs and KPIs to remain relevant and effective.

Example of OKRs and KPIs in FitSM:

- Objective: Improve the efficiency of the IT service management process.
    - KR1: Reduce the average resolution time for major incidents by 40%.

- o KR2: Increase the first-call resolution rate to 75%.
- KPIs:
  - o For KR1: Monitor the monthly average resolution time for major incidents.
  - o For KR2: Track the percentage of incidents resolved on the first call.

By integrating OKRs and KPIs into your FitSM implementation, you create a powerful mechanism for setting ambitious goals, tracking progress, and ensuring operational excellence. This approach not only drives strategic improvements but also ensures that these improvements are grounded in operational reality and effectiveness.

Monitoring and Communication:

Progress Monitoring utilizing Established OKRs and KPIs:

- Tracking with KPIs: Utilize the established Key Performance Indicators (KPIs) to continuously monitor the operational effectiveness of the FitSM processes. These KPIs provide measurable data points to assess how well the processes align with the defined objectives.
- Reviewing OKRs: Regularly review the progress against the established Objectives and Key Results (OKRs). This review should focus on evaluating how

the implementation is advancing towards achieving the broader strategic goals set in the OKRs.

Feedback Mechanisms:

- Creating Feedback Channels: Develop channels for gathering feedback from users and stakeholders regarding the newly implemented processes. This could involve surveys, suggestion boxes, or regular meetings.
- Incorporating Feedback into Continuous Improvement: Use the feedback received to inform continuous improvement efforts. This feedback is vital for understanding the impact of the changes and for making necessary adjustments to both processes and objectives.

By actively utilizing the established OKRs and KPIs for progress monitoring and creating effective feedback mechanisms, your organization can ensure a dynamic and responsive approach to the FitSM implementation. This strategy not only aids in tracking operational efficiency but also aligns process performance with strategic objectives, fostering a culture of continuous improvement and adaptation.

Effective Communication and Documentation:

- Clear Communication: Communicate the changes, their purposes, and benefits to all stakeholders.

Ensure that everyone understands the reasons behind the implementation and the expected outcomes.

- Accessible Documentation: Make sure that all documented processes are easily accessible. This could be through an internal knowledge base, intranet, or a dedicated FitSM documentation portal.

Support and Training:

Guidance and Support:

- Support Structures: Provide adequate support to your team during the initial stages of implementation. This could include help desks, FAQs, or dedicated support personnel.
- Addressing Challenges: Be prepared to address challenges or resistance proactively. Offer solutions and alternatives to ease the transition for team members.

Ongoing Training:

- Training Sessions: Conduct regular training sessions to ensure that all team members are proficient in the new processes. Include both theoretical and practical aspects in the training.

- Refresher Courses: Offer refresher courses or updates when processes are modified or new features are added.

Continuous Improvement:

Regular Review and Refinement:

- Iterative Improvement: Regularly review the implemented processes to identify opportunities for improvement. Use the feedback and data collected to refine and optimize processes.
- Adaptation to Change: Be flexible and ready to adapt processes in response to changing organizational needs, technological advancements, or feedback from stakeholders.

Celebrating Successes:

- Acknowledging Achievements: Recognize and celebrate the successful implementation of processes. This helps in building momentum and encouraging team morale.
- Sharing Success Stories: Share success stories and case studies within the organization to demonstrate the positive impact of FitSM implementation.

By strategically implementing FitSM processes and controls, monitoring progress, providing support, and continuously improving based on feedback, your organization can effectively integrate FitSM into its IT service management practices. This approach ensures not only the successful adoption of FitSM but also its sustained effectiveness and relevance in your organization's ITSM landscape.

Step 12: Leverage the Right Tools and Technologies

Evaluate your current tools and technologies to ensure their compatibility with FitSM. Identify any necessary upgrades or new tools that align with the framework's principles. Seek integrated tools that support the key processes in IT service management, such as incident and problem management, change management, configuration management, and service level management.

Automation is an essential aspect of achieving efficiency and consistency in service management, so prioritize tools that enable automation, reporting, and collaboration. Ensure that these tools provide the required functionality while also being user-friendly and adaptable to your organization's needs.

Evaluating Current ITSM Tools:

Compatibility Assessment:

- FitSM Alignment: Assess your current ITSM tools to ensure they align with FitSM principles. This involves evaluating whether the tools support the framework's processes and objectives.

- Gap Analysis: Conduct a gap analysis to identify any shortcomings in your current toolset that might hinder effective FitSM implementation.

Upgrades and New Tools:

- Identifying Requirements: Based on the gap analysis, identify the requirements for upgrades or new tools. Consider the specific needs of key FitSM processes.
- Vendor Evaluation: When selecting new tools or upgrades, evaluate vendors for their compatibility with FitSM, focusing on features, scalability, and integration capabilities.

Integrating Tools for Key ITSM Processes:

Supporting Core Processes:

- Incident and Problem Management: Choose tools that offer robust functionalities for logging, tracking, and resolving incidents and problems efficiently.
- Change Management: Look for tools that facilitate smooth change management processes, including change requests, impact analysis, and approval workflows.
- Configuration Management: Ensure tools can manage and track configuration items effectively, maintaining an accurate configuration management database (CMDB).

- Service Level Management: SLA Tracking and Reporting: Implement tools that can monitor and report on service level agreements (SLAs), ensuring compliance and facilitating communication with stakeholders.

Emphasizing Automation and Collaboration:

Automation for Efficiency:

- Automated Workflows: Prioritize tools that offer automation capabilities to streamline workflows, reduce manual errors, and increase efficiency.
- Reporting Automation: Utilize tools that can automatically generate reports for performance tracking, compliance, and strategic decision-making.

Collaboration Features:

- Team Collaboration: Choose tools that enhance collaboration among ITSM teams, including features for sharing information, joint problem-solving, and communication.

User-Friendly and Adaptable Solutions:

Ease of Use:

- User-Friendly Interface: Select tools with intuitive interfaces to ensure they are user-friendly, reducing the learning curve for your team.

- Training and Support: Ensure that the tool vendors provide adequate training and support for their products.

Adaptability to Organizational Needs:

- Customization Options: Look for tools that offer customization options to tailor them to your organization's specific needs and processes.
- Scalability: Ensure that the tools are scalable, capable of growing and adapting as your organization's needs evolve.

By carefully evaluating and selecting the right tools and technologies, you can significantly enhance the effectiveness of your FitSM implementation. The right set of tools not only supports the key processes of IT service management but also aligns with the overall objectives of efficiency, consistency, and adaptability within your organization.

Step 13: Pilot Implementation

Before implementing FitSM organization-wide, conduct a pilot implementation in a controlled environment. This enables you to test the framework's compatibility with your organization's specific needs and address any potential issues or challenges before full- scale implementation. The pilot phase provides an opportunity for feedback and learning, allowing you to make necessary adjustments, refine processes, and build confidence among stakeholders. Assess the outcomes of the pilot implementation against defined KPIs to determine its effectiveness and pinpoint areas for improvement.

Planning the Pilot Implementation:

Selecting the Pilot Area:

- Identify a Suitable Department or Team: Choose a department or team within your organization that is representative of the larger operations but contained enough to manage effectively. This could be a department that is particularly receptive to change or one that has been experiencing ITSM challenges.
- Scope Definition: Clearly define the scope of the pilot, including which FitSM processes will be tested and the duration of the pilot phase.

Setting Objectives and KPIs:

- Pilot Objectives: Establish clear objectives for the pilot implementation. These should align with your broader FitSM goals.
- Key Performance Indicators (KPIs): Define specific KPIs for the pilot phase to measure its effectiveness. These KPIs should provide quantifiable metrics to assess the pilot's success.

Executing the Pilot:

Implementing FitSM Processes:

- Process Rollout: Begin by implementing the selected FitSM processes within the pilot area. Ensure that these processes are aligned with the overall FitSM framework and adapted to the specific context of the pilot area.
- Monitoring and Support: Provide continuous monitoring and support throughout the pilot phase. This includes addressing any technical issues, process queries, and providing guidance to the involved team members.

Feedback and Learning:

- Gathering Feedback: Actively collect feedback from the participants involved in the pilot. This feedback is crucial for understanding the practical implications of the FitSM implementation.
- Learning and Adaptation: Use the insights gained from the pilot to make necessary adjustments. This learning phase is critical for refining processes before a wider rollout.

Assessing the Pilot Outcomes:

Evaluating Against KPIs:

- Performance Analysis: Assess the outcomes of the pilot implementation against the predefined KPIs.

Analyze whether the objectives of the pilot were met and to what extent.

- Identifying Successes and Challenges: Document the successes and challenges encountered during the pilot phase. This will provide valuable insights for the full-scale implementation.

Readiness for Broader Implementation:

- Decision Making: Based on the pilot outcomes, decide whether your organization is ready for a full-scale FitSM implementation. Consider whether additional pilots or adjustments are needed.
- Stakeholder Confidence: Use the results of the pilot to build confidence among stakeholders. Demonstrating success in a controlled environment can be a powerful tool for gaining broader organizational buy-in.

Preparing for Full-Scale Rollout:

Incorporating Lessons Learned:

- Process Refinement: Refine the FitSM processes based on the pilot experience. Ensure that the lessons learned are integrated into the framework for the broader implementation.
- Training and Communication: Update training materials and communication plans to reflect the insights gained from the pilot phase.

Scaling Up:

- Strategic Expansion: Plan for a strategic expansion of the FitSM implementation across the organization. This should include a detailed rollout plan, resource allocation, and a timeline for the full-scale implementation.

By conducting a pilot implementation, your organization can test and refine the FitSM framework in a controlled environment, ensuring that it is well-tailored to your specific needs and challenges. This step is crucial for mitigating risks, enhancing stakeholder confidence, and laying a solid foundation for a successful organization-wide implementation of FitSM.

Step 14: Communicate and Train

Regularly communicate the progress of the FitSM implementation to all stakeholders, keeping them informed about milestones achieved and upcoming changes. Address any concerns or questions that arise during the process promptly.

Provide ongoing training and support to users and stakeholders, ensuring their understanding and adoption of FitSM principles and processes. Encourage feedback and create channels for suggestions, fostering a sense of ownership and continuous improvement among stakeholders. Foster a collaborative culture where individuals feel empowered to share their perspectives and contribute to the success of the implementation.

Effective Communication Strategies:

Regular Updates:

- Progress Reports: Regularly update all stakeholders on the progress of the FitSM implementation. This includes sharing milestones achieved, upcoming changes, and any adjustments to the plan.
- Transparent Communication: Maintain transparency throughout the process. Clearly communicate both successes and challenges, fostering trust and credibility.

Addressing Concerns:

- Prompt Responses: Address any concerns, questions, or feedback that arise during the implementation process promptly and effectively.
- Feedback Mechanisms: Establish dedicated channels, such as regular meetings or digital platforms, where stakeholders can voice their concerns and provide feedback.

Ongoing Training and Support:

Comprehensive Training Programs:

- Tailored Training Sessions: Provide ongoing training sessions tailored to different roles and levels within the organization. This should cover both the theoretical aspects of FitSM and its practical application.

- Interactive Learning: Incorporate interactive elements such as workshops, simulations, and Q&A sessions to enhance engagement and understanding.

Support Structures:

- Help Desks and Support Teams: Set up help desks or support teams that stakeholders can reach out to for assistance with FitSM-related queries or challenges.
- Resource Availability: Ensure that training materials, guides, and resources are readily available and easily accessible to all users.

Fostering a Collaborative Culture:

Encouraging Stakeholder Feedback:

- Open Channels for Suggestions: Create and maintain open channels for stakeholders to submit suggestions and ideas. This could include digital suggestion boxes, dedicated email addresses, or regular brainstorming sessions.
- Acting on Feedback: Demonstrate that feedback is valued by acting on it where appropriate and

providing updates on how suggestions have been implemented or considered.

Empowerment and Ownership:

- Empowering Individuals: Foster a culture where individuals feel empowered to share their perspectives and contribute to the FitSM implementation process.
- Recognition and Involvement: Recognize and celebrate the contributions of stakeholders. Involve them in decision-making processes where possible, enhancing their sense of ownership and commitment to the project.

Continuous Improvement and Adaptation:

Iterative Learning and Improvement:

- Learning from Experience: Use the insights and feedback gathered during training and communication activities to continuously improve the FitSM implementation process.
- Adapting to Change: Be prepared to adapt training and communication strategies in response to evolving needs, challenges, and organizational changes.

By regularly communicating progress, addressing concerns, providing comprehensive training and support, and fostering a collaborative culture, your organization can enhance the understanding, adoption, and successful implementation of FitSM. This approach not only ensures effective stakeholder engagement but also promotes a culture of continuous improvement and shared responsibility for the success of the FitSM initiative.

Step 15: Review and Continuously Improve with OKRs and KPIs

Implementing a Dynamic Review Process:

Regular Evaluation with OKRs and KPIs:

- Balanced Review Approach: Utilize both Objectives and Key Results (OKRs) and Key Performance Indicators (KPIs) in your regular review sessions. While KPIs provide operational performance metrics, OKRs help in aligning these metrics with broader strategic goals.
- Stakeholder Engagement: Involve key stakeholders, including the project team, process owners, and end-users, in the review process to ensure a comprehensive evaluation of the FitSM implementation.

Feedback Integration and Action Planning:

- Feedback Collection: Actively gather feedback on the effectiveness and efficiency of the implemented processes. Encourage stakeholders to provide insights and suggestions for improvement.

- Actionable Insights: Analyze feedback in the context of your OKRs and KPIs. Develop action plans to address identified issues, aligning them with the strategic objectives and operational metrics.

Continuous Refinement and Strategic Alignment:

Adaptive Improvement:

- Iterative Refinement: Continuously refine and enhance your FitSM implementation based on ongoing reviews and feedback. Ensure that your practices remain adaptable to changing business needs, industry trends, and technological advancements.
- Innovation and Creativity: Promote a culture of innovation in service management, encouraging continuous learning and improvement.

Strategic and Operational Alignment:

- OKRs for Strategic Goals: Regularly revisit and adjust your OKRs to ensure they stay aligned with the organization's evolving strategic goals.
- KPIs for Operational Excellence: Use KPIs to monitor and analyze specific aspects of IT service management, such as incident resolution times, service availability, change success rates, customer satisfaction, and SLA compliance.

Leveraging OKRs and KPIs for Informed Improvements:

Informed Decision-Making:

- Data-Driven Analysis: Utilize the data from KPIs and the progress on OKRs to make informed decisions about resource allocation, process adjustments, and strategic direction.
- Trend Analysis and Benchmarking: Analyze trends and benchmark against industry standards to identify areas for improvement and innovation.

Ensuring Compliance and Effectiveness:

- Regular Audits and Assessments: Conduct audits or assessments to ensure ongoing compliance with FitSM requirements and to evaluate the effectiveness of the ITSM processes.
- Alignment with Business Objectives: Continuously ensure that both your OKRs and KPIs are aligned with the business objectives, facilitating a cohesive approach to IT service management.

By incorporating both OKRs and KPIs in the continuous review and improvement process, your organization can maintain a robust, responsive, and strategically aligned FitSM implementation. This approach not only tracks operational efficiency but also ensures that IT service management is consistently contributing to the broader goals of the organization.

Step 16: Communicate and Promote FitSM

Communication and promotion are crucial to the success and adoption of FitSM within your organization. Proactively communicate with your team members and stakeholders, keeping them informed about the progress of the FitSM implementation, upcoming changes, and expected outcomes.

Regularly share success stories, case studies, and best practices from within your organization to showcase the positive impact of FitSM. Celebrate achievements and milestones, acknowledging the efforts of individuals and teams involved in the implementation.

Consider creating a communication plan that outlines the key messages, communication channels, and target audiences.

Leverage various communication channels, including emails, newsletters, intranet portals, team meetings, and town hall sessions, to reach out to your stakeholders effectively.

Engage champions and influencers within your organization to advocate for FitSM and encourage adoption. Encourage open and transparent communication, providing avenues for feedback and ideas from all levels within your organization.

Step 17: Seek External Support and Certification

If desired, seek external support and certification to validate your FitSM implementation and demonstrate your commitment to IT service management best practices. External consultants or assessors can provide expert guidance, assess your FitSM implementation against industry standards, and identify areas for improvement.

Consider pursuing ISO/IEC 20000 certification, which provides an internationally recognized validation of your IT service management practices. ISO/IEC 20000 is a globally accepted standard that aligns with the principles and requirements of FitSM. Certification can enhance your organization's credibility, provide a competitive advantage, and demonstrate your commitment to delivering high-quality IT services.

Conclusion

Implementing FitSM is a step-by-step process that requires planning, collaboration, and continuous improvement. By following this guide, you will be equipped with the knowledge and tools necessary to lay a solid foundation for FitSM within your organization. Remember to tailor FitSM to your organization's needs, involve key stakeholders, and regularly review and refine your implementation to ensure its long-term success.

CHAPTER 5

THE DARK SIDES OF FITSM:

NAVIGATING POTENTIAL PITFALLS

While Fitsm offers numerous advantages for organizations seeking to streamline their IT service management practices, it is not without its challenges. Like any framework or methodology, FitSM has its potential pitfalls. This chapter delves into the less-discussed aspects of FitSM, shedding light on the potential dark sides and offering guidance on how to navigate them effectively.

5.1 Over-Reliance on Standardization

The Pitfall: One of the primary objectives of FitSM is to standardize IT service management processes. However, an over-reliance on standardization can stifle innovation and flexibility, leading to a one-size-fits-all approach that may not cater to the unique needs of every department or business unit.

Navigating the Challenge: It's essential to strike a balance between standardization and customization. While core processes can be standardized, allow room for departments to tailor certain aspects to their specific needs.

5.2 Complexity in Large Organizations

The Pitfall: In large, multi-departmental organizations, the implementation of FitSM can become complex, leading to confusion and misalignment.

Navigating the Challenge: Establish a centralized task force or committee responsible for overseeing the FitSM implementation. This team should ensure consistent communication and alignment across all departments.

5.3 Overemphasis on Documentation

The Pitfall: While documentation is a critical aspect of FitSM, an overemphasis on it can lead to bureaucracy, slowing down processes and decision-making.

Navigating the Challenge: Focus on creating concise, relevant, and actionable documentation. Avoid the trap of documenting for the sake of documentation.

5.4 Potential for Inflexibility

The Pitfall: The structured nature of FitSM can sometimes lead to inflexibility, making it challenging for organizations to adapt to rapidly changing business environments.

Navigating the Challenge: Encourage a culture of continuous improvement. Regularly review and update FitSM processes to ensure they remain relevant and agile.

5.5 Cost Implications

The Pitfall: The initial implementation of FitSM can be resource-intensive, requiring investments in training, tools, and possibly even new hires.

Navigating the Challenge: Consider the long-term benefits of FitSM against the initial costs. While there may be upfront expenses, the long-term gains in efficiency, productivity, and customer satisfaction can outweigh these costs.

5.6 Misalignment with Other Frameworks

The Pitfall: Organizations that use multiple frameworks may find some aspects of FitSM conflicting with other methodologies they have in place.

Navigating the Challenge: Ensure that there's a clear understanding of how FitSM integrates with other frameworks. Where conflicts arise, prioritize processes that align with the organization's broader objectives.

Conclusion

FitSM, like any other framework, is a tool. Its effectiveness largely depends on how it's implemented and integrated into an organization's culture and processes. By being aware of potential pitfalls and proactively addressing them, organizations can harness the full power of FitSM while minimizing its dark sides.

CHAPTER 6

CASE STUDIES:
SUCCESSFUL FitSM IMPLEMENTATION

In this chapter, we will delve deeper into real-world case studies of organizations that have implemented FitSM and compare their experiences with those that have implemented ITSM. These case studies serve as valuable sources of inspiration and learning for businesses embarking on similar journeys and provide insights into the benefits, challenges, and differences between the two frameworks, offering a more comprehensive analysis.

CASE STUDY 1

COMPANY A - FitSM IMPLEMENTATION FOCUSING ON
SERVICE LEVEL MANAGEMENT AND CHANGE
MANAGEMENT

Background:

Company A, a medium-sized technology firm, embarked on a journey to adopt FitSM to align its service management practices with agile development methodologies. The firm sought a framework that was both efficient and adaptable to its dynamic service environment.

Implementing Service Level Management (PR2):

Assessment and Alignment:

Company A conducted a thorough assessment of their existing service management practices, identifying gaps in service level agreements (SLAs) and performance monitoring. They aligned their SLAs with FitSM's Service Level Management requirements, ensuring they were realistic, measurable, and aligned with customer expectations.

Engagement and Training:

The firm engaged employees across departments, emphasizing the importance of meeting SLAs and how it contributes to customer satisfaction. Training sessions were conducted to familiarize teams with the new SLA processes and metrics, fostering a service-oriented culture.

Benefits Realized:

› The implementation of FitSM's Service Level Management led to more transparent and achievable SLAs, enhancing customer satisfaction.

› Regular reviews of service performance against SLAs allowed for continuous improvement in service delivery.

Implementing Change Management (PR12):

Integrating with Agile Practices:

› Company A integrated FitSM's Change Management process with their existing agile development practices. This integration ensured that changes were managed systematically while retaining agility.

› The Change Advisory Board (CAB) was established, comprising representatives from various departments, to evaluate and approve significant changes.

Streamlining Change Processes:

› The firm adopted a more streamlined approach to managing changes, with clear roles and responsibilities defined as per FitSM guidelines.

› Automated tools were introduced to track and manage change requests, ensuring a transparent and efficient process.

Outcomes of Effective Change Management:

› The new change management process led to fewer service disruptions and a more predictable IT environment.

› Employees embraced the structured yet flexible approach to change, aligning it with the firm's agile ethos.

Conclusion:

Company A's transition to FitSM, with a particular focus on Service Level Management and Change Management, exemplifies the framework's adaptability and effectiveness in a dynamic service environment. By aligning their service management practices with FitSM's principles, Company A not only enhanced its service delivery and customer satisfaction but also embraced a culture of continuous improvement and agility. This case study demonstrates the practical benefits of FitSM in a real-world setting, particularly for organizations seeking to integrate service management with agile methodologies

CASE STUDY 2

COMPANY B - TRANSFORMATION WITH ITSM:
CHALLENGES AND TRIUMPHS

Company B, a large financial institution, recognized the value of a comprehensive framework that includes well-defined processes, roles, and responsibilities. They decided to implement ITSM to standardize service management processes across multiple departments and ensure compliance with regulatory requirements.

The implementation of ITSM at Company B presented several challenges due to the organization's complex operations and hierarchies. Resistance to change, lack of stakeholder buy-in, and the need for extensive training and education were some of the significant hurdles faced by the organization. The process of aligning existing processes with the ITSM framework required significant time and effort, necessitating clear communication and involvement from all levels of the organization.

ITSM provided Company B with a structured and comprehensive approach to service management. The clearly defined processes, roles, and responsibilities helped standardize service delivery across departments and improved overall service quality. The implementation of ITSM enhanced accountability, as employees understood their specific roles and responsibilities within the framework, and transparency increased across the organization.

However, the rigidity of ITSM presented challenges when the organization needed to deviate from predefined processes or adapt to changing market conditions. This inflexibility caused delays and inefficiencies, requiring additional efforts to optimize the framework and align it with the specific needs of the business. Despite these challenges, the comprehensive nature of ITSM brought long-term benefits to Company B, ensuring consistency across departments and improving service quality across the organization.

While the implementation and maintenance costs associated with ITSM were higher compared to FitSM, Company B recognized the value of the investment in having a standardized and comprehensive framework in place. They were able to achieve better control and governance of their service management practices, ensuring compliance with regulatory requirements and building customer trust through consistent service delivery.

CASE STUDY 3

COMPANY C - GLOBAL FITSM IMPLEMENTATION:
BRIDGING DIVIDES FOR UNIFIED SERVICE EXCELLENCE

Background and Objectives:

Company C, a multinational in the telecommunication sector, faced challenges in unifying IT service management across its diverse and geographically dispersed operations. The primary goals of implementing FitSM were to standardize service delivery processes, enhance customer satisfaction, and achieve cost efficiencies.

Implementation Strategy:

Cross-Functional Implementation Team: Company C formed a team comprising IT professionals, change management experts, and business representatives from various regions. This diversity ensured that the strategy accommodated different operational nuances.

Addressing Change Resistance: The team encountered resistance to change and the complexity of aligning various business units under a standardized framework. They tackled these challenges through robust change management strategies and stakeholder engagement.

Utilizing OKRs and KPIs:

Setting Strategic OKRs:

› Objective 1: Achieve a unified standard in IT service management across all regions.

   o KR1: Implement FitSM framework in 75% of business units within one year.

   o KR2: Attain at least 90% compliance with standardized processes in implemented units.

› Objective 2: Enhance overall customer satisfaction.

- o KR1: Improve customer satisfaction scores by 20% post-implementation.

Operational Excellence with KPIs:

› Incident Resolution Time: Monitored the average time taken to resolve incidents, aiming for a significant reduction.

› Service Availability: Assessed the percentage of time services were available to users, striving for minimal downtime.

› Change Success Rate: Tracked the success rate of changes implemented, aiming for minimal disruptions.

Implementation Journey and Challenges:

› Effective Change Management: Regular communication, training sessions, and workshops were integral in managing resistance and fostering a culture of collaboration and acceptance.

› Monitoring and Continuous Improvement: Continuous monitoring of OKRs and KPIs helped identify areas needing improvement and facilitated quick corrective actions.

Outcomes and Successes:

Achievements:

› Company C observed a marked reduction in incident response times and an increase in customer satisfaction, indicating improved service quality.
› The implementation led to optimized resource allocation and cost savings.

Learning and Adaptation:

› The journey highlighted the importance of stakeholder involvement and the role of change champions.
› Regular reviews of OKRs and KPIs provided valuable insights, enabling ongoing refinement of processes and strategies.

Cultural Shift:

› The successful implementation fostered a culture of continuous improvement and innovation within the company.

Conclusion:

Company C's experience demonstrates the effectiveness of FitSM in standardizing IT service management across a multinational landscape. The strategic use of OKRs and KPIs was pivotal in aligning operational activities with broader organizational goals, driving success in service management, and fostering a culture of continuous improvement and customer-centricity. This case study serves as a practical example for organizations looking to leverage FitSM, emphasizing the importance of comprehensive planning, stakeholder engagement, and the judicious use of performance metrics.

CASE STUDY 4

COMPANY D - DIGITAL LEAP WITH FITSM: AUTOMATION, ANALYTICS, AND ENHANCED SERVICE DELIVERY

Background and Objectives:

Company D, a prominent financial institution, embarked on a journey to modernize its ITSM practices in line with the evolving business landscape and customer expectations. Their goal was to enhance agility, scalability, and efficiency in IT service delivery through the implementation of the FitSM framework.

Strategic FitSM Implementation:

In-Depth ITSM Evaluation:

Conducted a comprehensive assessment of existing ITSM practices, identifying key areas for improvement. Focused on aligning ITSM practices with FitSM's modular and scalable structure to meet specific organizational needs.

Adopting Automation and Analytics:

› Service Catalog Automation (Service Portfolio Management - PR1): Implemented an automated service catalog, enhancing the user experience and streamlining service request fulfillment.

› Workflow Automation (Change Management - PR12): Utilized analytics and automation tools to automate key workflows, reducing manual intervention and accelerating service delivery.

Enhancing Incident and Problem Management:

Proactive Incident Management (Incident and Service Request Management - PR9):

› Established enhanced monitoring and alert systems to proactively detect and address potential incidents.

› Implemented automated incident categorization and prioritization to improve response times.

Effective Problem Resolution (Problem Management - PR10):

› Emphasized root cause analysis to reduce recurrence of incidents.

› Developed a structured approach to problem resolution, ensuring a higher level of service availability and reliability.

Achievements and Impact:

Operational Efficiency and Customer Satisfaction:

› Observed a significant reduction in service outages and improved service quality metrics.
› Enhanced customer experience through more efficient and responsive IT services.

FitSM Principles in Action:

› Demonstrated the successful application of FitSM principles in a financial institution, showcasing the framework's adaptability to different industry settings.
› Leveraged FitSM's focus on efficiency and customer-centricity to drive improvements in IT service management.

Conclusion:

Company D's FitSM journey highlights the transformative impact of integrating advanced ITSM practices with a focus on automation, analytics, and proactive service management. By aligning their ITSM practices with FitSM's principles and leveraging technology tools, Company D achieved notable improvements in operational efficiency, service quality, and customer satisfaction. This case study serves as a testament to the effectiveness of FitSM in enhancing IT service management, particularly in sectors where compliance, security, and customer trust are paramount.

CASE STUDY 5

COMPANY E - FITSM TRANSFORMATION: BOOSTING EFFICIENCY & SATISFACTION

Background and Objectives:

Company E, a medium-sized manufacturing firm, embarked on a journey to optimize their IT service management practices. Their objectives were to standardize IT processes, enhance inter-departmental communication and collaboration, and boost overall productivity.

Strategic Implementation of FitSM:

Formation of a Dedicated Task Force: A task force comprising IT professionals, business representatives, and change management experts was established. This team conducted a thorough analysis of the organization's unique challenges to develop a customized FitSM implementation plan.

Focus on Service Desk and SLA Management:

> Establishing a Centralized Service Desk (Incident and Service Request Management - PR9): Company E set

up a service desk as the central point of contact for all IT-related service requests and inquiries.

› The service desk was equipped with tools and processes to provide prompt and effective support, significantly enhancing user satisfaction.

Adopting and Monitoring SLAs (Service level management - PR2):

› The firm introduced clear service level agreements (SLAs) to set and manage service quality expectations. Regular monitoring and reporting against these SLAs were implemented to ensure service consistency and identify areas for continuous improvement.

Achievements and Cultural Shift:

Operational Efficiency and Customer Satisfaction:

› The implementation of a centralized service desk led to a more efficient handling of service requests, reducing downtime and improving response times. The clear definition and monitoring of SLAs contributed to a consistent service experience, enhancing customer satisfaction.

Organizational Benefits

> Strong leadership support and active employee engagement were key drivers in the successful adoption of FitSM.

> The firm fostered a culture of continuous improvement, leading to improved operational efficiency and customer satisfaction.

Conclusion:

Company E's FitSM transformation journey demonstrates the effectiveness of implementing structured IT service management processes in a manufacturing context. By focusing on establishing a centralized service desk and adopting robust SLA management, the company was able to standardize its IT processes, improve inter-departmental collaboration, and enhance overall productivity. This case study serves as an insightful example for other organizations aiming to integrate FitSM into their business improvement strategies, highlighting the importance of tailored implementation, strong leadership, and a culture of continuous improvement.

CASE STUDY 6

COMPANY F - FITSM JOURNEY: ENHANCING IT SERVICE SECURITY AND COMPLIANCE

Background and Goals:

Company F, a provider of technology solutions, recognized the need to bolster compliance and security within their IT service management practices. Their primary objectives were to enhance data protection, minimize security risks, and manage IT service delivery effectively, aligning with industry best practices and regulatory requirements.

Strategic Implementation of FitSM:

Initial Assessment and Gap Analysis: Conducted an in-depth assessment of their existing IT infrastructure and processes. Identified vulnerabilities and gaps, particularly in areas related to security and compliance.

Establishing a Governance Framework (General Requirements - GR1, GR2):

Developed a comprehensive governance framework, including policies, procedures, and controls. Ensured alignment with regulatory standards and industry frameworks, such as ISO 27001.

Focus on IT Service Continuity and Security:

IT Service Continuity and Disaster Recovery (Service Availability and Continuity Management - PR4): Implemented robust service continuity and disaster recovery plans to mitigate potential disruptions.

Established mechanisms to ensure business continuity, including regular testing and updates of the plans.

Security and Compliance Measures (Information Security Management - PR6):

Integrated stringent security measures into IT service management practices.

Regularly updated security protocols to address evolving threats and maintain compliance with industry standards.

Monitoring and Continuous Improvement:

Regular Audits and Evaluations: Conducted regular audits to verify compliance with the established governance framework. Evaluated the effectiveness of security measures and identified areas for continuous improvement.

Achievements in Security and Compliance: Observed a significant reduction in security incidents and data breaches. Improved incident response times, enhancing overall IT service resilience and reliability.

Conclusion: Company F's FitSM journey underscores the framework's effectiveness in establishing a secure and compliant IT service management environment. By focusing on IT service continuity, disaster recovery planning, and stringent security measures, Company F not only aligned with regulatory requirements but also enhanced its overall service delivery. This case study highlights the importance of a structured approach to ITSM, particularly in areas of security and compliance, and demonstrates how FitSM can be instrumental in achieving a robust security posture and ensuring business continuity in the technology sector.

CASE STUDY 7

COMPANY G - HEALTHCARE REVOLUTION: ENHANCING PATIENT CARE WITH FITSM INTEGRATION

Company G, a large hospital network, recognized the impact that efficient and effective IT service management could have on patient care. They embarked on a FitSM journey to improve IT service delivery, optimize clinical workflows, and enhance overall patient experience.

To ensure the success of the implementation, Company G developed a comprehensive ITSM strategy tailored to the specific needs of the healthcare industry. They engaged clinical staff, IT professionals, and administrators throughout the process to gather insights and ensure alignment with patient care goals.

One of the key areas of focus for Company G care was the integration of ITSM principles into clinical processes, such as patient registration, diagnostic tests, and medication administration. By streamlining these processes, Company G significantly reduced waiting times, improved care coordination, and enhanced patient satisfaction.

Additionally, they leveraged FitSM to implement a robust incident management system, allowing quick identification and resolution of IT issues that could impact patient care. By minimizing disruption to critical systems and equipment, Company G ensured seamless healthcare services delivery.

Through their commitment to FitSM implementation, Company G witnessed improved patient outcomes, increased operational efficiency, and standardized processes across their network of hospitals. This case study highlights the transformative power of FitSM in the healthcare sector, where ITSM plays a crucial role in delivering quality patient care.

Conclusion

These case studies provide detailed insights into the successful implementation of FitSM and ITSM principles across various industries and organizational sizes.

Comparing FitSM and ITSM in the first two case studies highlights key differences between FitSM and ITSM, which organizations should carefully consider when deciding on the most suitable framework for service management implementation.

FitSM offers a lightweight and flexible approach suitable for organizations with agile development methodologies and a focus on speed and adaptability. The modular structure of FitSM allows for customization and scaling to meet specific needs, resulting in cost savings. Its user-friendly nature facilitates better understanding and acceptance among employees, reducing resistance to change. The agility of FitSM allows organizations to respond quickly to changing customer requirements and market demands.

On the other hand, ITSM's structure and strict processes cater to organizations with complex operations and compliance requirements. The comprehensive nature of ITSM ensures consistency across departments and improves service quality.

However, the rigidity of ITSM can sometimes hinder agility and require additional efforts to adapt to unique business needs. While the overall implementation and maintenance costs of ITSM may be higher, the investment in a standardized and comprehensive framework can bring long-term benefits in terms of control, governance, and compliance.

The extended examples demonstrate the transformative power of FitSM implementation, including streamlining service delivery processes, improving customer satisfaction, ensuring compliance and security, and enhancing patient care in the healthcare industry.

Organizations must carefully assess their unique circumstances, goals, and preferences when considering FitSM or ITSM implementation. The lessons and insights from these case studies provide valuable guidance for making an informed decision on the most suitable framework for service management implementation. By studying these organizations' experiences and adapting their strategies to ft their own contexts, businesses can embark on a successful implementation of FitSM and ITSM principles with confidence. Here are some key takeaways and recommendations based on the case studies:

I. Stakeholder Involvement: Engaging stakeholders at all levels is crucial for the success of FitSM implementation. This includes IT professionals, business representatives, and change management experts. By ensuring diverse perspectives and active participation, companies can overcome resistance to change and foster a culture of collaboration.

2. Change Management: Effective change management strategies are essential for smooth FitSM implementation. Regular communication, training sessions, and workshops help create awareness, understanding, and acceptance of the new framework. Strong leadership support and clear communication of the benefits also play a vital role in driving successful change.

3. Automation and Analytics: Leveraging technology tools such as automation and analytics can significantly enhance the effectiveness of FitSM implementation. Automation minimizes manual intervention, streamlines processes, and reduces service delivery time. Analytics helps identify potential incidents proactively and enables proactive problem resolution.

4. Continuous Improvement: A culture of continuous improvement is critical for sustained success with FitSM implementation. Regular monitoring, reporting, and evaluation against predefined service level agreements (SLAs) ensure service consistency and provide insights for ongoing enhancements. Organizations should strive for regular audits to verify compliance and identify areas for improvement.

5. Alignment with Regulatory Standards: Integrating FitSM with relevant industry frameworks and

regulatory requirements ensures compliance and enhances data protection. Organizations should conduct thorough assessments and establish governance frameworks comprising policies, procedures, and controls. Regular audits and evaluations help in maintaining compliance.

6. Industry-Specific Tailoring: Adapting FitSM principles to the specific needs and requirements of the industry is vital for success. Organizations should consider the unique challenges and characteristics of their sector when developing their FitSM implementation strategies. This will enable them to achieve the desired outcomes and maximize the benefits of FitSM.

In summary, these case studies demonstrate the remarkable impacts and benefits that organizations can achieve through the successful implementation of FitSM and ITSM principles. By learning from the experiences of the companies in our case studies, businesses can gain valuable insights and guidance for their own FitSM journeys. Customizing the implementation strategies to their specific needs, engaging stakeholders, fostering a culture of continuous improvement, and leveraging technology tools will enable businesses to optimize their IT service management practices and drive overall business success.

CHAPTER 7

FUTURE OF FITSM:

EMERGING TRENDS AND

OPPORTUNITIES

I n this chapter, we will delve deeper into the future of FitSM and explore the emerging trends and opportunities in the field of IT service management. FitSM has gained recognition and popularity due to its simplicity and practicality in managing IT services. As organizations continue to evolve and adapt to the ever-changing digital landscape, it is crucial to understand the potential directions that FitSM may take and the opportunities it can offer.

7.1. Emerging Trends

7.1.1. Integration of Artificial Intelligence and Machine Learning

One of the most significant emerging trends in FitSM is the increasing integration of artificial intelligence (AI) and machine learning (ML) technologies. AI and ML have the potential to revolutionize IT service management by automating routine tasks, enhancing problem- solving capabilities, and improving decision- making processes. Organizations are leveraging AI and ML in various ways within the FitSM framework:

a. Intelligent Service Desk: AI-powered chatbots and virtual assistants can provide instant and intelligent support to customers, minimizing response times and improving customer satisfaction. These chatbots can understand and interpret customer queries, provide relevant solutions, and perform automated tasks, freeing up human agents to handle more complex issues.

b. Predictive Analytics: AI and ML algorithms can analyze vast amounts of IT service management data to predict potential issues, identify patterns, and suggest proactive measures. By leveraging these predictive analytics capabilities, organizations can prevent service disruptions, reduce downtime, and optimize resource allocation. By applying AI techniques, organizations can optimize resource allocation, respond to incidents more swiftly, and improve overall service quality and availability. AI is also revolutionizing ITSM through predictive analytics, enabling proactive problem management, and assisting with root cause analysis.

c. Automation plays a crucial role in streamlining ITSM processes by reducing manual effort and enabling organizations to achieve greater efficiency and accuracy. It eliminates mundane and repetitive tasks, such as incident logging or service request fulfillment, allowing IT professionals to focus on strategic initiatives that add value to the organization.

d. Automated Incident Management: AI and ML technologies can automate incident management processes by identifying patterns in incident data, suggesting troubleshooting steps, and even performing automated resolutions. This automation expedites the incident resolution process and minimizes the impact on services.

7.1.2 Agility and Flexibility

The future of FitSM also lies in the focus on agility and flexibility in IT service management. With rapid technological advancements and changing customer demands, organizations need to be agile in their service delivery. FitSM provides a framework that allows organizations to adapt and respond quickly to new requirements and market trends. To enhance agility in the FitSM framework, organizations are adopting the following practices:

a. Agile Methodologies: Organizations are integrating agile methodologies such as Scrum or Kanban within the FitSM framework to drive innovation, optimize processes, and deliver value to their customers more effectively. These methodologies enable incremental and iterative development, ensuring quicker time to market and continuous improvement.

b. DevOps Integration: The integration of DevOps practices within FitSM is gaining momentum. DevOps aims to bridge the gap between development and operations teams, enabling faster development cycles, improved collaboration, and more reliable service delivery. By adopting DevOps principles and practices within the FitSM framework, organizations can achieve faster time to market, higher quality releases, and improved customer satisfaction.

c. Cloud and Hybrid Environments: As organizations increasingly adopt cloud and hybrid IT environments, FitSM provides a flexible foundation for managing these environments effectively. FitSM allows organizations to adapt to changing infrastructure needs, scale services seamlessly, and leverage the benefits of cloud technologies.

7.1.3. Service Integration and Management (SIAM)

With the increasing reliance on multiple service providers and the growing complexity of IT landscapes, SIAM has emerged as a critical theme in FitSM implementation. SIAM focuses on managing the end-to-end delivery of services across multiple service providers, ensuring seamless integration and coordination of service delivery.

SIAM principles provide organizations with guidance on establishing clear roles and responsibilities, communication channels, and governance structures between service providers and the organization. They ensure that all involved parties work collaboratively towards a common goal, ensuring effective management of service delivery.

The implementation of SIAM practices enables organizations to navigate complex service provider ecosystems, ensuring service levels and performance targets are met. It helps to establish effective governance structures and service-level agreements (SLAs) with service providers, ensuring accountability and transparency.

SIAM also promotes effective collaboration amongst service providers, enabling seamless integration of services and avoiding potential gaps or overlaps. It focuses on end-to-end service management, enabling organizations to deliver a consistent and cohesive service experience to their customers.

By implementing SIAM practices within FitSM, organizations can enhance service quality, minimize service disruptions, and improve customer satisfaction by ensuring the seamless integration and coordination of service delivery across service providers.

7.1.4. Integration of Cybersecurity

Another trend shaping the future of FitSM is the increased emphasis on cybersecurity. As the digital landscape becomes more complex and interconnected, organizations face an ever- growing number of cybersecurity threats. FitSM can provide a robust foundation for implementing stringent cybersecurity practices, ensuring the confidentiality, integrity, and availability of IT services. Integration of cybersecurity within the FitSM framework includes:

a. Secure Service Design: FitSM facilitates a secure service design approach, ensuring that security considerations are embedded from the initial stages of service development. By integrating security controls and best practices, organizations can mitigate risks proactively and prevent potential vulnerabilities.

b. Security Incident Management: FitSM emphasizes effective management of security incidents to minimize their impact. Organizations integrate incident response plans, security monitoring, and threat intelligence within the FitSM framework to detect and respond swiftly to security incidents.

c. Compliance and Regulatory Requirements: FitSM helps organizations meet compliance and regulatory requirements by providing guidelines and controls that ensure adherence to industry standards and regulations. By integrating compliance management within FitSM, organizations maintain the trust of their stakeholders and safeguard sensitive data.

7.2 Opportunities

The future of FitSM presents several opportunities for organizations looking to enhance their service management capabilities and deliver exceptional customer experiences. By leveraging emerging technologies, embracing agile methodologies, and prioritizing cybersecurity, organizations can differentiate themselves from competitors and stay ahead in a rapidly evolving digital landscape.

7.2.1 Innovation and Competitive Advantage

By adopting FitSM and its emerging trends, organizations can drive innovation, optimize processes and services, and gain a competitive advantage in the market. Leveraging AI and ML technologies within FitSM can lead to enhanced service delivery and personalized customer experiences, setting organizations apart from their competitors. Organizations can explore the use of AI in data analysis, automation, and decision-making processes to unleash their innovative potential.

7.2.2 Enhanced Collaboration and Communication

The integration of DevOps practices within the FitSM framework fosters enhanced collaboration and communication between development and operations teams. This collaboration ensures alignment and synergy among different stakeholders, leading to improved service delivery and faster resolution of issues. By enabling cross-functional collaboration, organizations can break down silos, promote knowledge sharing, and foster a shared sense of ownership for service delivery, ultimately enhancing overall communication and teamwork.

7.2.3 Improved Risk Management and Compliance

With the increasing focus on cybersecurity, FitSM offers organizations the opportunity to improve their risk management and compliance practices. By integrating stringent cybersecurity measures into the FitSM framework, organizations can proactively identify and mitigate risks, ensuring regulatory compliance and minimizing potential breaches. Organizations can leverage FitSM's security controls and guidance to assess and manage risks effectively, enhancing the overall resilience and protection of their IT services.

7.2.4 Enhanced Customer Satisfaction

FitSM's focus on agility, automation, and customer-centricity enables organizations to deliver exceptional customer experiences. By adopting FitSM and its emerging trends, organizations can respond quickly to changing customer demands, deliver services with higher efficiency, and create personalized experiences for their customers, leading to increased customer satisfaction and loyalty. Organizations can leverage automation, AI- powered self-service options, and predictive analytics to deliver proactive and personalized services, ultimately enhancing the overall customer experience.

Conclusion

The future of FitSM holds promising trends and opportunities for organizations embarking on their IT service management journeys. Embracing and leveraging these future trends in FitSM and ITSM will be essential for organizations to stay competitive in the evolving digital landscape. The integration of AI and ML technologies, the emphasis on agility and flexibility, the adoption of DevOps practices, and the prioritization of cybersecurity will shape the future landscape of FitSM:

- Automation and AI technologies will continue to enhance the efficiency and effectiveness of FitSM and ITSM processes, enabling proactive problem management and improving customer support through virtual agents and chatbots.
- The shift towards cloud-based service management will provide organizations with greater scalability, flexibility, and real-time visibility into service performance. Self-service portals will empower customers and reduce the burden on IT teams.

- Integration between FitSM, ITSM, and DevOps methodologies will drive faster time-to- market and high-quality service delivery through collaboration and automation. SIAM will play a vital role in managing multi-vendor and multi-sourced IT environments, ensuring seamless coordination and consistent service delivery.
- Security and privacy will be critical considerations, with organizations adopting a holistic approach and embedding secure practices into every aspect of FitSM and ITSM. Compliance with data protection regulations will be essential.
- Customer experience and service design will take center stage, with organizations leveraging customer feedback and insights to personalize services and enhance the overall customer journey. Advanced analytics and AI technologies will enable organizations to deliver targeted recommendations and drive customer loyalty.

By staying abreast of these emerging trends and embracing new opportunities, organizations can leverage FitSM to achieve their strategic objectives, adapt to evolving customer demands, achieve business growth in the digital era, and thrive in an increasingly competitive digital landscape.

CHAPTER 8

TIPS FOR SUCCESSFUL FITSM

IMPLEMENTATION

I mplementing FitSM successfully requires careful planning and execution. Here are some essential tips to ensure a smooth and effective implementation:

Gain Management Support:

To begin your FitSM implementation journey, it is crucial to obtain strong support from top- level management. Management support serves as the foundation for successful implementation, as it ensures their endorsement and involvement throughout the process. By securing their commitment, you can acquire the necessary resources, authority, and funding to implement FitSM effectively. Additionally, management support reinforces the importance of FitSM adoption across the organization, encouraging staff to embrace and actively participate in the implementation.

Establish Clear Objectives:

Before diving into the implementation process, it is essential to define clear objectives for FitSM. These objectives should align with the organization's overall strategy and goals. By clearly articulating what you aim to achieve with FitSM, you set a direction for the implementation efforts and enable stakeholders to understand and align their efforts with the broader organizational vision. Clear objectives also serve as a measuring stick for success, enabling you to track progress and evaluate the impact of FitSM adoption.

Conduct a Readiness Assessment:

A thorough readiness assessment is crucial to identify existing strengths, weaknesses, and challenges within the organization. Evaluate various aspects such as existing IT service management (ITSM) processes, IT infrastructure, organizational structure, and culture. This assessment enables you to determine the organization's readiness for FitSM adoption and highlights areas that may require additional attention, adaptation, or potential barriers to successful implementation. Comprehending these factors allows you to anticipate potential limitations, plan effectively, and ensure a seamless transition to FitSM.

Customize FitSM:

FitSM is designed as a flexible framework that can be customized to ft the unique needs and characteristics of your organization. While the core principles and processes remain consistent, tailoring FitSM to suit your organization's specific size, industry, available resources, and service management maturity is essential. Through customization, you can enhance adoption and alignment of the framework with existing organizational practices, avoiding unnecessary disruptions and ensuring a better ft.

Consider modifying elements such as roles and responsibilities, processes, or documentation templates to ensure FitSM integrates seamlessly into your organization's operations.

Develop a Comprehensive Implementation Plan:

A well-structured and comprehensive implementation plan is a vital tool for successful FitSM adoption. It provides a roadmap that outlines the necessary steps, allocated resources, timeline, and milestones required to achieve your objectives. The well- defined plan should clearly identify key activities such as stakeholder engagement, staff training, process design, tool selection, and communication strategies. By breaking down the implementation process into manageable phases and setting realistic timelines, you can effectively manage the implementation, monitor progress, and mitigate potential risks.

Engage and Train Staff:

Implementing FitSM is a collective effort that requires engagement and buy-in from staff at all levels of the organization. Actively involve stakeholders from various departments and ensure their input in the process. Communication and education play a crucial role in creating awareness and understanding the benefits of FitSM. Conduct training sessions, workshops, and information sessions to help staff comprehend the FitSM framework, their roles, and responsibilities within it. Openly discuss any concerns, answer questions, and emphasize the positive impact FitSM will have on the organization. Engaged and knowledgeable staff are more likely to embrace FitSM and contribute to its successful implementation.

Pilot and Test:

Before implementing FitSM organization-wide, it is advisable to conduct a pilot phase to test and validate the framework's effectiveness in a controlled environment. Select a representative sample of processes, teams, or departments and implement FitSM practices in collaboration with involved stakeholders. This pilot phase allows you to identify any potential challenges, gather feedback, and make necessary adjustments before a full-scale implementation. It provides an opportunity to fine-tune procedures, assess the feasibility of proposed changes, and identify potential areas for improvement. Learning from the pilot phase will enhance the chances of a successful and seamless organization-wide implementation.

Monitor and Measure:

Implementing FitSM is a dynamic and ongoing process that necessitates continuous evaluation and improvement. To effectively measure the success of FitSM implementation, it is essential to establish both Key Performance Indicators (KPIs) and Objectives and Key Results (OKRs).

KPIs should focus on quantitatively assessing the efficiency and effectiveness of the newly implemented practices. These metrics might include customer satisfaction rates, incident resolution times, service availability, and other critical IT service-related metrics. KPIs provide a clear, measurable way to track performance against operational goals.

In parallel, OKRs should be set to align these operational metrics with the organization's broader strategic objectives. OKRs enable the setting of ambitious goals (Objectives) with specific, measurable outcomes (Key Results) that reflect the organization's vision and aspirations in implementing FitSM. For instance, an

Objective could be to enhance overall IT service agility, with Key Results including measurable improvements in service deployment times or reductions in incident recurrence rates.

Regular monitoring of both KPIs and OKRs is crucial. This dual approach ensures not only that the day-to-day operations are aligned with the FitSM framework but also that these operations contribute to the larger strategic goals of the organization. By tracking these metrics, areas for improvement can be identified, allowing for data-driven decisions to continually optimize the FitSM implementation.

This method of using both KPIs and OKRs fosters a balanced approach to IT service management, ensuring that tactical efficiency is achieved without losing sight of strategic growth and improvement. It encourages a culture of continual progress, where operational successes contribute to achieving broader business objectives.

Communicate and Celebrate Success:

Effective communication plays a critical role in successful FitSM implementation. Regularly communicate updates, progress, and milestones achieved to all stakeholders in the organization. Emphasize the benefits and positive impact FitSM is bringing to the organization, highlighting improvements in service delivery, customer satisfaction, and operational efficiency. Celebrate key achievements and milestones to recognize collective effort and dedication. By celebrating success, you create a positive atmosphere that reinforces the importance of FitSM adoption and encourages ongoing commitment and support from staff.

Continuous Improvement:

FitSM implementation is not a one-time task but an ongoing process of continuous improvement. Foster a culture that encourages staff to identify areas of improvement, challenge existing practices, and propose enhancements to the FitSM framework. Regularly review and assess the effectiveness of implemented processes, tools, and documentation.

Conduct periodic audits to ensure compliance and alignment with FitSM principles. Encourage collaboration and knowledge- sharing between teams to promote cross-functional learning and the exchange of best practices. By embracing a culture of continuous improvement, you enable the organization to evolve and optimize its IT service management practices, thereby maximizing the value derived from FitSM implementation.

Ensure Scalability and Flexibility:

As your organization grows and evolves, it is crucial to ensure that the FitSM implementation can scale and adapt accordingly.

Regularly review the ft between FitSM and your organization's changing needs and make necessary adjustments. Consider incorporating feedback from stakeholders and incorporating new technologies or industry best practices. Embrace an agile approach that allows for flexibility and responsiveness to emerging business requirements. By ensuring scalability and flexibility, you can sustain the value derived from FitSM implementation in the long term.

Foster a Culture of Collaboration:

Successful FitSM implementation relies on fostering a culture of collaboration across the organization. Encourage cross- functional teams to work together, sharing knowledge and expertise to improve IT service management practices. Promote open communication channels that facilitate the sharing of challenges, ideas, and solutions. Establish communities of practice or forums where employees can exchange insights and learn from one another. By nurturing a culture of collaboration, you enable your organization to leverage collective intelligence and drive continuous improvement in FitSM adoption.

Leverage Automation and Technology:

Automation and technology play a vital role in optimizing IT service management practices and maximizing the benefits of FitSM implementation. Explore opportunities to leverage tools, platforms, and technologies that support FitSM processes and enhance efficiency.

Consider implementing a service management tool that aligns with FitSM principles, providing automation for incident management, change management, or service level management. Automation can streamline processes, reduce manual effort, and improve accuracy, enabling your organization to focus on delivering high-quality IT services.

Engage External Support:

If your organization lacks internal resources or expertise for implementing FitSM, consider engaging external support such as consultants or trainers. External support can provide valuable insights, knowledge, and experience in FitSM implementation.

External support can assist with various aspects of the implementation process, including gap analysis, process design, training, and change management. Consultants can provide guidance on how to align FitSM with industry best practices and tailor it to your organization's specific needs.

They can also help navigate any challenges or roadblocks that may arise during implementation, drawing on their expertise and experience from other successful FitSM implementations.

Engaging external support can also help accelerate the implementation timeline, as consultants bring a fresh perspective and specialized knowledge that can expedite the process. They can provide training to staff on FitSM concepts and best practices, ensuring a smooth transition and effective adoption.

Additionally, consultants can conduct independent audits or assessments to evaluate the progress and effectiveness of FitSM implementation. Their objective and impartial perspectives can provide valuable insights and recommendations for further improvement.

When engaging external support, it is important to select reputable consultants or training providers that have proven experience with FitSM implementation. Look for certifications, customer testimonials, and case studies to gauge their expertise and track record.

In summary, external support can be a valuable resource to drive successful FitSM implementation. Their expertise, guidance, and support can help organizations overcome challenges, accelerate implementation, and optimize the benefits derived from FitSM adoption.

Conclusion

In conclusion, FitSM and ITSM are both valuable frameworks that organizations can leverage to improve their IT service management practices. While they may have some similarities, they also have distinct differences that make each framework unique.

FitSM focuses on providing a lightweight, flexible, and practical approach to IT service management. One of the key aspects of FitSM is its simplicity, allowing for easy adoption and implementation. By streamlining complex processes, FitSM enables organizations to establish efficient and effective IT service management practices without unnecessary bureaucratic burden. FitSM's principles are centered around delivering value to the business, fostering continuous improvement, and optimizing the use of resources.

The FitSM framework is designed to support organizations of all sizes and industries. It provides guidance on areas such as service management strategy, service design, service operation, and continual service improvement. FitSM emphasizes the importance of agility and adaptability, enabling organizations to respond quickly to changing business needs and market demands.

On the other hand, ITSM is a more standardized and comprehensive framework, providing organizations with a structured set of processes and practices. ITSM frameworks such as ITIL (Information Technology Infrastructure Library) offer detailed guidance on best practices for various aspects of IT service management. These frameworks have been widely adopted by organizations around the world and have proven to be effective in enhancing service delivery and support.

ITSM frameworks provide a holistic approach to IT service management, covering areas such as service strategy, service design, service transition, service operation, and continual service improvement. Organizations adopting ITSM frameworks gain access to a wealth of knowledge and expertise, ensuring that their IT services are aligned with the needs of the business and delivered efficiently and effectively.

While FitSM may lack the depth and breadth of ITSM frameworks like ITIL, its simplicity and flexibility make it an excellent choice for smaller organizations or those looking for a more lightweight approach to IT service management. FitSM's focus on practicality and value delivery ensures that organizations can obtain quick wins and tangible benefits from its implementation.

However, it is important to consider the specific needs and context of your organization before deciding between FitSM and ITSM. Factors such as the size of the organization, complexity of IT infrastructure, industry requirements, and organizational culture can influence the choice of framework.

For enterprise-level organizations with complex IT environments, ITSM frameworks may provide a more comprehensive and structured approach to service management. The detailed processes and practices offered by ITSM frameworks can benefit organizations by standardizing operations, enhancing efficiency, and driving continuous improvement.

On the other hand, smaller organizations or those with less complex IT landscapes may find FitSM to be a better ft due to its simplicity and flexibility. FitSM's lightweight approach allows for easier implementation, especially for organizations with limited resources or those in the early stages of IT service management maturity.

Regardless of the framework chosen, implementing FitSM or adopting ITSM practices requires careful planning, stakeholder alignment, and continuous improvement. It is crucial to have a clear understanding of the strengths and limitations of each framework and tailor the implementation accordingly.

Organizations should consider conducting a thorough assessment of their current IT service management practices and identify areas for improvement or gaps that need to be addressed. This assessment will help organizations determine whether FitSM or an ITSM framework is the most appropriate choice.

Moreover, organizations should also involve key stakeholders throughout the implementation process. Engaging stakeholders such as IT teams, business units, customers, and senior management will ensure buy-in and support for the chosen framework. By involving stakeholders, organizations can gather valuable insights, address concerns or resistance, and align the IT service management strategy with broader organizational objectives.

Finally, continuous improvement is essential for maintaining and enhancing IT service management practices. Whether following FitSM or an ITSM framework, organizations should regularly review and assess their IT service management processes, identify areas for optimization, and implement changes accordingly. This continual service improvement approach will allow organizations to adapt to evolving business needs, address emerging challenges, and deliver increased value to their customers.

Ultimately, FitSM and ITSM are powerful tools that organizations can leverage to enhance their IT service management practices. Both frameworks provide valuable guidance and best practices to optimize service delivery and support. The choice between FitSM and ITSM ultimately depends on the specific needs and requirements of your organization. By implementing these frameworks effectively, organizations can enhance their IT service management capabilities and deliver better value to their customers.

APPENDIX A GLOSSARY OF TERMS

To fully understand and navigate the world of FitSM and ITSM, it is essential to familiarize yourself with the various terms and concepts commonly used in this field. This

chapter provides an extended glossary of the key terms that you will come across in your journey towards implementing FitSM and ITSM successfully.

1. **Activity:** Set of actions carried out within a process.
2. **AI (Artificial Intelligence):** Artificial Intelligence, often abbreviated as AI, refers to the development of computer systems that can perform tasks that typically require human intelligence. These tasks may include problem-solving, learning, reasoning, speech recognition, language understanding, and visual perception. AI technologies can be categorized into two main types: Narrow AI, which is designed for specific tasks, and General AI, which aims to replicate human-like intelligence across a wide range of activities. AI is used in various fields, including healthcare, finance, autonomous vehicles,

natural language processing, and robotics, to enhance efficiency and provide innovative solutions.

3. **Change Management:** Change management is the process of controlling and implementing changes to the IT infrastructure in a controlled and systematic manner. It aims to minimize the impact of changes on service quality and ensure that changes are implemented in a predictable and reliable fashion. This includes assessing and approving change requests, planning and scheduling changes, and communicating and documenting the changes' impacts. Change management focuses on maintaining stability and control in the face of evolving business needs and technological advancements.

4. **COBIT (Control Objectives for Information and Related Technologies):** COBIT is a framework for the governance and management of enterprise IT. It provides a set of principles, practices, and guidelines for organizations to ensure that their IT investments are aligned with business objectives, managed effectively, and comply with regulatory requirements. COBIT focuses on areas such as risk management, control frameworks, and the measurement of IT performance to enable better decision-making and governance of IT resources.

5. **Configuration Management:** Configuration management involves the identification, control, and governance of the components, configurations, and relationships of the IT infrastructure. It provides a comprehensive understanding of the configuration items (CIs) and their interdependencies to enable effective change and incident management. This includes maintaining accurate records, managing configuration baselines, and conducting regular audits to ensure the integrity of the configuration data. Configuration management ensures that the IT infrastructure is reliable, secure, and aligned with the organization's business requirements.

6. **Continual Service Improvement (CSI):** CSI is an ongoing process of reviewing and improving IT service management practices to ensure they align with the changing needs of the business. It involves analyzing performance data, identifying areas for improvement, and implementing corrective actions. CSI fosters a culture of continuous learning and innovation, driving enhancements in service quality, efficiency, and cost-effectiveness. By regularly assessing and adapting IT service management practices, organizations can achieve greater effectiveness, optimize resource utilization, and enhance customer satisfaction.

7. **DevOps (Development and Operations):** DevOps is a set of practices and cultural philosophies that aim to improve collaboration between software development (Dev) and IT operations (Ops) teams. It seeks to automate and streamline the software delivery and infrastructure management processes, enabling organizations to release software faster, with higher quality, and more reliability. DevOps emphasizes principles such as continuous integration, continuous delivery (CI/CD), automation, infrastructure as code (IaC), and monitoring. By breaking down silos and fostering a culture of collaboration and communication, DevOps helps organizations deliver software products more efficiently and respond quickly to customer needs.

8. **FitSM (Federated IT Service Management):** FitSM is a lightweight, standards-based approach to IT service management. It offers organizations a structured and practical framework to establish and maintain effective IT service management practices. FitSM focuses on ensuring that services meet customer needs and are aligned with business objectives by employing a flexible and tailored approach.

9. **Incident Management:** Incident management is the process of restoring normal service operation as

quickly as possible following an incident. It involves the identification, recording, classification, investigation, and resolution of incidents that disrupt the normal functioning of services. The primary goal is to minimize the impact of incidents on the business and its users. Incident management focuses on timely and effective restoration of service, with a strong emphasis on customer satisfaction and minimizing the negative impact on business operations.

10. **ISO 20000:** ISO 20000 is an international standard for IT service management (ITSM). It outlines the requirements for establishing, implementing, maintaining, and continually improving an ITSM system. ISO 20000 is based on ITIL principles and helps organizations demonstrate their commitment to delivering high-quality IT services. Compliance with ISO 20000 can lead to improved service delivery, customer satisfaction, and operational efficiency, making it a valuable framework for organizations seeking to enhance their IT service management practices.

11. **ITIL (Information Technology Infrastructure Library):** ITIL is a framework of best practices for managing IT services and aligning them with business needs. ITIL provides a structured approach to service management, with a focus on delivering value to

customers through effective service design, transition, operation, and continuous improvement. It defines processes and functions such as Incident Management, Problem Management, Change Management, and Service Level Management to ensure that IT services are delivered efficiently, with high quality, and in alignment with business goals.

12. **ITSM (IT Service Management):** ITSM refers to the set of activities, processes, and policies that are put in place to design, plan, deliver, operate, and control IT services. It encompasses the entire lifecycle of IT services, ensuring they align with business needs and objectives. The primary goal of ITSM is to deliver value to customers by providing quality IT services that support business operations efficiently and effectively.

13. **Kanban:** Kanban is a visual project management and workflow optimization system that originated from manufacturing but is now widely used in software development and other industries. Kanban boards visually represent work items and their progress through various stages of a workflow. It allows teams to manage work in progress (WIP), optimize flow, and focus on completing tasks efficiently. Kanban emphasizes the principle of limiting WIP to avoid overburdening team members and to ensure that

work items are completed more predictably and with higher quality.

14. **ML (Machine Learning):** Machine Learning is a subset of artificial intelligence that focuses on the development of algorithms and statistical models that enable computer systems to learn from and make predictions or decisions based on data. ML algorithms are designed to recognize patterns, discover insights, and make predictions without explicit programming. ML applications are wide-ranging, from image and speech recognition to recommendation systems, fraud detection, and autonomous vehicles. ML models learn and adapt over time as they are exposed to new data, making them valuable tools for data-driven decision-making.

15. **Policy:** Documented set of intentions, expectations, goals, rules and requirements, often formally expressed by top management representatives in an organization or federation.

16. **Problem Management:** Problem management focuses on preventing recurring incidents by identifying and addressing their underlying root causes. It involves proactive analysis and intervention to identify trends, conduct investigations, and implement long-term solutions. The aim is to minimize the impact of problems on service quality and ensure stable and reliable service

delivery. Problem management focuses on the overall health and stability of services, aiming to identify and eliminate underlying issues to prevent future incidents from occurring.

17. **Procedure:** Specified set of steps or instructions to be carried out by an individual or group to perform one or more activities of a process.

18. **Process:** Structured set of *activities* with clearly defined responsibilities that bring about a specific objective or set of results from a set of defined inputs.

19. **Scrum:** Scrum is a popular framework for agile project management and product development. It promotes collaboration, flexibility, and iterative progress in software development and other complex projects. In Scrum, work is organized into short time periods called sprints, typically lasting two to four weeks. During each sprint, a cross-functional team works to deliver a potentially shippable product increment. Scrum includes defined roles (Scrum Master, Product Owner, and Development Team), ceremonies (Daily Standup, Sprint Planning, Sprint Review, and Sprint Retrospective), and artifacts (Product Backlog, Sprint Backlog, and Increment) to facilitate effective teamwork and transparency.

20. **Service Catalog:** A service catalog is a comprehensive list of all the IT services that are available to customers. It provides detailed information about each service, including features, benefits, pricing, support options, and dependencies. The service catalog helps users understand and select the services that best meet their needs, facilitates service request management, and supports effective service-level agreements. Service catalogs improve transparency and communication between the service provider and the customer, enabling efficient management of services and enhancing customer satisfaction.

21. **Service Desk:** The service desk is a single point of contact for customers to report incidents, request services, and seek assistance. It serves as the primary communication channel between the service provider and the customers and enables efficient and timely handling of inquiries and support requests. Service desks may range in complexity and can provide self-help options, remote assistance, and escalation mechanisms. Service desks play a critical role in ensuring a positive customer experience, resolving issues promptly, and maintaining customer satisfaction.

22. **Service Level Agreement (SLA):** An SLA is a formal agreement between a service provider and a

customer that outlines the expected level of service delivery. It defines the performance targets, metrics, responsibilities, and remedies, ensuring clarity and transparency in the service relationship. SLAs play a crucial role in managing customer expectations, providing a basis for monitoring and reporting service performance, and establishing a mutual understanding between the service provider and the customer.

23. **Service Level Objective (SLO):** An SLO is a measurable target that defines the desired level of performance for a specific IT service. It specifies the expected level of availability, response time, resolution time, and other key performance indicators. SLOs are typically agreed upon between the service provider and the customer as part of the service level agreement and serve as a basis for monitoring and reporting service performance. SLOs provide a clear understanding of the expected service levels and serve as a benchmark for measuring and improving service delivery.

24. **Service Management:** Service management involves the coordination and control of activities and resources required to deliver valuable services to customers. It covers a wide range of practices and processes that contribute to the planning, design, transition, operation, and continuous improvement

of services. Service management is based on a customer-centric approach, where the focus is on meeting customer needs and expectations.

25. **Service management system (SMS):** Overall management system that controls and supports management of services within an organization or federation.

By familiarizing yourself with these terms, you will be better equipped to understand and implement FitSM and ITSM practices effectively. This extended glossary serves as a comprehensive reference, providing a solid foundation as you embark on your journey towards achieving streamlined and efficient IT service management.

APPENDIX B BIBLIOGRAPHY

- FitSM website: https://www.fitsm.eu/
- Measure What Matters by John Doerr
- Balanced Diversity: A Portfolio Approach to Organizational Change by Karen Ferris
- The Checklist Manifesto: How to Get Things Right by Atul Gawande
- ITIL Foundation Essentials ITIL 4 Edition by Claire Agguter
- Measuring ITSM by Randy A. Steinberg
- ITIL 4 High-velocity IT, by AXELOS

INDEX

.